theCoderBros GO TO WHITE CASTLE

A Lighthearted Asian American
Success Story

Hansel Lynn and Wayne Teng

theCoderBros
Go to White Castle

Published by:

AUTHORSon**MISSION**

Table of Contents

For Maile, Beck, Mathis, Ella, and Emma.

May you grow up to find your BFF with whom to share your own stupid adventures.

Introduction

June 13, 2022, Chase Center, San Francisco, California. Celtics at Warriors, the NBA Finals; this was for all the marbles. We're Hansel and Wayne – during any normal day, we'd be helping kids learn to code, but today we're having our minds blown in real-time by our team, the Golden State Warriors. This was the home clincher for the Warriors, the most critical home game of the entire season. Winning this game would leave them one more game to win to get the NBA championship.

We're seated just behind billionaire team owner Joe Lacob and his wife. Our seats were on the court itself, and we could feel the thump of the ball as Jayson Tatum dribbled by. Seated within spitting distance – not that we'd spit on him, but we didn't invent the phrase – is Jay Z. We're not billionaires, but we got the seats. This is absolutely insane to us. *Is this real?! We are so not worthy.* Because of a bit of luck, a little skill, and a lot of hard work, us two Chinese dudes were now sitting courtside at the priciest NBA stadium there is. We're midcourt, right next to the TV announcers at a game that's about to decide the fate of our team, sitting about five feet away from Steph Curry, the biggest name in basketball.

This game is us taking a break (sort of, we'll get to that later) from our company, theCoderSchool, to get in some Us Time. Not only do we run a company together, but we're also best friends. We're in the thick of it now, with the game unfolding all around us.

Poole is frantically waving his arms for the ball, and Wiggins passes to Poole with less than a second left on the clock. Hansel suddenly remembers that insane prime rib buffet from before the game and hopes desperately he doesn't have to take a massive dump before everything is over. Sure, the buffet is part of the ticket price, and true to our Chinese upbringing, we arrived early to get our money's worth. Suddenly, Poole just *sinks it* and boom! we're ahead by one. And no one needs to take a dump (as far as we know).

We've been high-fiving Nicole Curran (Joe Lacob's wife) all night, so in comes a barrage of hands from her. We slap the hell out of each other's palms, brimming with excitement. Steph Curry bounces on by – coming close enough to, well, spit on us – and, for about the hundredth time that night, because we sat so close, we're convinced he's coming our way to high five us. Wayne did once pat him on the back to wish him good luck in the tunnel before a game, a story we'll get to in due time.

As the Warriors win, the crowd jumps up, players leaping around the court in celebration. As the sports reporters on the floor try to yell above the din, everything feels like it's happening in slow motion. At least to us. Maybe Shawn (that's what we'd call Jay Z if we knew him) was used to this kind of thing. Not us. The camera flashes start popping off, the celebratory drinks are getting poured, and we're there just wondering *how we could possibly be here.* We both think back to growing up in small-town, white-white Middle America as Asian-American kids whose immigrant parents scraped by, only to be here. Now. In this moment. More importantly, in *the* moment.

If this were a movie, now's the part when we'd look at each other in slow-mo, and the picture would freeze on us just as a camera flash goes off, the sound echoing into the night. One of us would start talking over the scene and say, "I bet you're wondering how we got here," as the opening credits come flying on the screen.

If you squint really hard, our movie's a lot like the *Harold and Kumar* movie, where the climax to the stupid adventures of two Asian bros was finding their White Castle. Only our White Castle wasn't a fast-food joint, it was this amazing little small business called theCoderSchool. Here's a little story about two Chinese dudes who love Bruce Lee (and even met his flesh and blood, another story we'll get to later), don't mind making fun of their own, and legitimately crave eating White Castle in real life. It's a story about two best friends running a successful franchise business that was built from scratch and who not only loved, but lived, *Harold and Kumar Go to White Castle*. And don't forget to squint really hard. Unless you're Asian – then you're good.

Part 1

We Two Asians

Chapter 1

Hansel without Gretel

Life didn't start out with endless buffets and high-fives from famous people. Growing up in the Midwest meant that sort of thing, those amazing life events, were still a world away. I was born in Columbus, Ohio, probably to make sure I got my U.S. Citizenship, and soon after, we moved to Hong Kong to live with my grandma (or Popo, as the Cantonese say) until I was five. We then boomeranged back to the US, to Iowa where my uncle was a professor, to get an American education. Still, we headed back to Hong Kong every summer until I was in college, so my Popo could help raise me and teach me how to speak and be Chinese. I missed out on all the summer camps and fishing or whatever White folks did, but I became a true Hong Konger

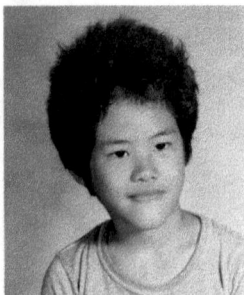

Hansel's awesome hair

from all that time there. It was in Hong Kong that I discovered the man I now call "The Bruce", the most bad-ass Hong Konger that ever lived.

I became a quiet kid after we moved to Iowa, probably from the shock of a new language and culture at such a young age. Quiet doesn't even begin to describe it.

No, I was a scared, nervous, socially awkward kid who struggled to interact with others. Someone should do a study on that – how many Asians just clam up when dropped into a new culture and language at a very young age? I'm not sure, I just know I was definitely one of them.

I was the kid who ate lunch alone in middle school because I didn't know how to talk to other kids. I remember once I was on a plane in high school, and a female human being from my class was on the same flight. She waved hi to me, and I literally froze and then pretended I didn't see her for the rest of the flight. Not easy when you're in a metal tube sitting across from someone for a few hours. This social awkwardness lasted a lot longer than you'd think – it wasn't until well after college that I felt like a normal person. Suffice it to say, I felt like a lonely outsider throughout my childhood (and part of adulthood), which is emotionally tough on a kid.

My dad died of unknown causes when my mom was pregnant with me, meaning I grew up without a father. And because of that, I had a mom that worked – a lot. The lack of a parental figure may have also contributed to my social ineptness. With my mom gone so often, the TV damn near raised me – I knew the TV schedule from 3:30 PM to 11 PM, backwards and forwards, from *Gilligan's Island* all the way to *Joanie Loves Chachi* and later. Ah, I miss the good old days before Instagram.

Iowa

I didn't have a lot of friends in Iowa. I felt self-conscious pretty often, and I never knew how to act around kids *or* adults. I had my posters and magazine collections of Bruce Lee (and I would talk to him *a lot*), and I had my two Iowan friends, Jay and Virgil. Jay looked like a shorter version of Roger Daltrey and was the one that got me into *The Who*. I even have a tattoo of the band's mod symbol on my left ankle to show for it. Virgil's a black guy who was one of the smartest kids in my uber-white high school in Iowa. He used to call me "Rynn" (like Lynn, but with an accent). Looking back, it was kinda racist but actually, hilariously awesome, too. In a way, the nickname made me feel like someone, like somehow, I was slightly cool. Virgil's such an Iowan, he once excitedly told me he found this awesome, rare, and new kitchen appliance that... cooked rice. If you don't get that joke, it's ok – you're not Asian.

Now, I *did* say I grew up without a dad, but I can't say I didn't have a father figure. My older brother, Haniel, had the job of watching over me. He was only a year older, but his mentor status was pretty clear, in hindsight. He was voted most likely to succeed (which he did and is now the successful CEO of a $200 million dollar company after graduating from UPenn/Wharton), and has always been there for advice, and even the occasional boost when it came to getting theCoderSchool launched decades later.

My mom's name is Hannah. This Hong Kongese family of three living in white-as-can-be Iowa is confusing enough as is it, and then we had to be named Hannah, Haniel, and Hansel? Haniel's name apparently came from the Bible – although before the age of the internet, we could never find it there. As for my name, Hansel, my mom simply said it rhymed with Haniel. Years later, I learned it means 'a gift for luck in new ventures' in Old English. It may not have felt like it early on (it felt more like everyone always made fun of the name – "Where's Gretel?!?"), but maybe it was a sign that I'd be a successful entrepreneur someday, after getting over my crippling shyness. Haniel, on the other hand, was a born leader. He was that popular-crowd valedictorian kid in school who helped take care of me while my mom busted her ass at McDonald's when we first moved back to the US. You gotta do what you gotta do to survive, including flipping burgers. It turned out well though, she eventually moved on to becoming a very successful and well-respected social worker.

Haniel had an Apple 400 computer when I was in 5th or 6th grade. I remember playing a Bruce Lee video game on it, one that you had to load from cassette tape. I eventually figured out how to code on it on my own, and the first thing I built was a drawing program (they didn't call them "apps" back then), like a super rudimentary Microsoft Paint. Honestly, I was pretty impressed with myself – they didn't have YouTube or even coding books for kids back then, you just had to figure it out. I kept going, and eventually programming a computer became the first and probably only thing I felt I was good at when I was young.

In high school, I took a computer science class (yep, they had those in Iowa in the 80s). My teacher, Mr. Dennis Johnson, told me I was good at programming, and even called me the Wiz. I would code my assignment in 3 minutes when it took the class the entire hour. So, I kept practicing and getting better. The thing is, I thought I was probably good, but when a teacher says that you're good to your face, it hits home (so thank you, Mr. Johnson!). Suddenly it's real and becomes not only the thing I'm destined to major in at college, but also the thing my career would eventually be based on. That's the powerful impact of a good teacher.

WashU

Wayne and I went to the same college at Washington University in St. Louis, but he was 4 years ahead of me, so we never met there. By college age, I'd finally discovered this magical concept called "other Asian people," while Wayne was still doing his own thing (i.e., hanging out with White people). Back in Des Moines in 1980, it was white. Bright, blinding, white. But at a highly ranked college like WashU, the Asians come out of the woodwork. I was in yellow heaven, going to the Asian parties where everyone looked like me, and suddenly feeling like I belonged. It was the start of finding myself and figuring out how to just *talk* to people like a normal person. I even started to find a slice of hipster inside me when I started twirling my Chinese hair into dreadlocks – like Jeremy Lin's, but even cooler (and about 25 years earlier). The clam was starting to open, ever so slowly.

Life is funny that way. Some folks mature early, I matured much later. But that's ok – life is about improving anything and everything, constantly. I was a kid who couldn't talk to people and would sweat buckets in class presentations. I now do keynote speeches next to U.S. Congresspersons and have no problem chatting with big celebrities (I just met Andrew Luck the other day – awesome dude). As a high schooler, I was literally the last kid to finish the mile run. Now I do Ironman triathlons. And no one who knew me would have ever pegged me to be a successful entrepreneur – but today I can say I founded, built, and run a pretty amazing company that's changed a lot of lives.

They say life is a journey. Awkward introvert to CEO might not be a typical journey, but however hard it was for me early on, I'll take the end result any day – floor seats at the NBA Finals with my best friend Wayne.

Chapter 2

Wayne's World

To borrow from Steve Martin's *The Jerk*, I was born a poor black child. Well - yellow child, actually. And I had plenty of rich white people around me to make me a little self-conscious about it. I was born in St. Paul, Minnesota, surrounded by blonde Scandinavians. My family left Minnesota when I was three to head to Alabama, but for some reason I still root for the Vikings. I guess you have to have a home team.

My brother, Sandy, is four years older, so he got all the Minnesota memories, including the awesome German Shepherd we had that I only know from stories. Yes, even our dog was European. When we got to Alabama, things were a little different, at least in terms of high paying tech jobs. Huntsville, nicknamed 'Rocket City', was where NASA built the rockets that took humans to the moon. But like Minnesota, it was home to a lot of the same types of folks – white people.

In 1980, Huntsville had over 300,000 residents, but only about 300 were Chinese. Most Chinese residents were immigrants who had strong accents. As one of the few American-born Chinese, I didn't have one – and that made me feel more like I belonged. It started with my parents, who decided they wouldn't teach Chinese to us, so we could blend right in (sort of) to White America. Sure, I wasn't anxious and awkward like Hansel, but I also never really built an attachment to Chinese culture and language, something I miss as an adult. At least I can still count on Hansel for ordering food at the Chinese restaurants.

The Family

I grew up in a family of five. Me, my brother Sandy, little sister Sue, and mom and dad. Sue looked like a perfect China doll growing up with long, straight black hair. Sandy and I though both had these kung-fu

Wayne (far right) and family

mullets – straight bangs in the front and long as hell in the back. It was like a lazy bowl cut, where you've stopped halfway through. It was so long that our grandma thought she had three granddaughters when she came to visit – a pretty one and two really fugly ones.

My dad was a character. He was a math and aerospace genius with a big personality. If the most famous person in the world walked into the room, he would've introduced himself. This is how he got deals done. Big government deals. He once got a million-dollar government contract (huge amount for the day), and it made the paper for being the biggest government contract with a minority. It turns out he wasn't exactly a business genius, and that company eventually went bankrupt. Asians, take note that a good career isn't just about math and science.

My mom was the stable one. She had to hold down the fort as a registered nurse. My dad was always traveling and busy trying to launch new businesses (unfortunately, none of them ended up taking off), so I spent much more time with my mom who was always around and taking care of us kids and the household. Late in her life, I would return that favor by having her live with us and taking care of her, like any good Asian son.

High School Transition

My family didn't have a lot of money growing up. But with Huntsville in a tech boom, there was plenty of money around me. I ended up at a school that felt like *Clueless*, with rich white people everywhere. Only this was the South, so the pretty girls there were what you'd call debutantes. I did my damnedest to make my way in amongst them, and to my surprise, most liked me. To them, I probably fit right in, thanks to Mom and Dad not giving me a Chinese accent (although my kung-fu mullet didn't help).

Of course, all I could see were the differences. I was wearing Sears and K-Mart jeans, and they were on top of all the trends. I remember one girl wearing Gloria Vanderbilt jeans – I told her I liked them, and she told me that *they had a name*. Wait, you name your pants? Suddenly it hit me – oh crap, everyone has brands!

What brand are mine? I've got Payless shoes, and everyone's got Marty McFly Nikes on. Even everyone's underwear had brands, and none of them had even heard of Fruit of the Loom.

When my mom heard about my fashion troubles, she started stashing away cash so I could have a Ralph Lauren shirt. She even pulled in military friends to take care of me – they get good deals at the PX on base, so they could get her stuff a little cheaper. She was an awesome Asian Mom, always trying to make my transition to a not-Chinese-world easier.

And Huntsville, Alabama was definitely not a Chinese world. It was this hidden tech center of the country, with some kids heading to the Ivy Leagues and other kids burning their necks red. I'd be out with friends, and some random dude would just make a Bruce Lee noise, and I'd be forced to think about how I didn't look like my friends. Someone even called me a Chink from across the field once during gym class, and no one even batted an eye.

I remember once being compared favorably to a girl who had come to school straight from Taiwan. She spoke no English yet and had an accent when she tried. Someone complimented me on how much better my English was than hers. I remember thinking, "Of course it is. I'm an American! I was born here!" But they can't see that, and some people can only operate off of what they see. The purely ignorant ones are hard to hate, because they'll just say something stupid, and the next thing you know, they're handing you a pecan pie. Good people can be ignorant. That's just how this stuff goes.

As for me, I luckily wasn't picked on too much. Probably because my parents made me as American as they could from the start, and probably because I've always been fairly athletic, too. That was also thanks to my parents – my dad got my brother and me into tennis early enough that we'd go on to play varsity in college. My dad passed when I was in my 30s, but he loved tennis so much that his tombstone reads, "Playing tennis in heaven!"

I was so American that, unlike Hansel, I had dated plenty in high school and college – all white girls. I always pictured myself in a John Hughes movie – that was the romance I wanted. It was either that or Long Duk Dong in *Sixteen Candles*, which wasn't exactly the best representation of Asian characters. Whether I only dated white girls because that's all there were around me, or whether that's who I liked, I don't know. I just know that it worked out pretty well for me in high school.

All in all, my transition to white America was pretty smooth. I ended up developing a close-knit group of friends at Randolph High School who I mostly stay in touch with to this day. Shout out to my white boys Sloyer, Yarb, Morgan, Tulio, Shockman, and Pendergrass. An extra shout out to Amit, who was the only Asian in the group (Indian, but close enough).

Superman

My first Asian buddy, Amit, would be the connection to my first experience with a celebrity. After undergrad, I went to LA to get my master's degree at USC. Amit was there, too, working. He was one of those geniuses from Huntsville who went to an Ivy school (Princeton), and his roommate was Dean Cain. Dean, at the time, was also in LA, living that celebrity life. He was, after all, TV's Superman. Parties, hot dates, other celebrities – Amit and I lived the star life vicariously through Dean. We were guests at MTV parties, hung out in his trailer, and even met celebrities like Teri Hatcher and Dean's many girlfriends like Ami Dolenz, Pamela Anderson, and Gabrielle Reece. And to the surprise of the Hollywood uninitiated like us, everyone, including Dean himself, was super cool and down-to-earth.

I always had a secret dream of being an actor but never pursued it, so I guess this would have to do unless you count the fact that I'd been doing plenty of acting as a white dude in an Asian body. That is, until I met Hansel.

Chapter 3

When Asian Worlds Collide

We were on opposite coasts before we met in the 90s. After WashU, Hansel was in DC for a job as a programmer, and Wayne was in LA, partying with Dean Cain. We both had computer science degrees and had decent enough, if not uninspiring, software jobs. Wayne went from USC to government contract work at TRW, and Hansel spent some time at Andersen after SAIC. No, you don't need to know these companies or what they did. If you did, you'd think we were at some boring-ass companies getting some good but not great paychecks, and you'd probably be right. Imagine our tech jobs as scenes from *The Office*, but with all the mundane parts and none of the humor.

Bros at First Sight

Fast forward a few years to 1997, when we both moved to the Bay Area to work for Cambridge Technology Partners, an up-and-coming systems consulting company. Consulting offered excitement through travel and the opportunity to build innovative software projects for large companies.

One of the consulting projects we both ended up at early on was at Hewlett-Packard in Cupertino. Wayne was a project manager there when Hansel was staffed as a coder. On Hansel's first day, from across a crowded room of yuppy consultants, Wayne walked into the slow-motion strains of "Dream Weaver" as Hansel looked up from his keyboard. "I bet I'm gonna be friends with this guy," he said. Wayne was, after all, the only other Asian guy Hansel's age on this whole project. As these things go, though, it wasn't to be. Not yet. Wayne moved to another project almost immediately, so the friendship would have to wait.

Actually, hold on a second; that's not when we met at all. Not as Wayne remembers it. Wayne thinks we met when someone else got a group together to go out for drinks, and Hansel brought his girlfriend. Hansel doesn't remember that, and said it definitely wasn't him since he'd never had a girlfriend by that point. Must have been some other Asian dude. See, even Asians can't tell themselves apart.

However it began, Wayne does remember that our friendship grew through a lot of snowboarding. Group trips, guy trips, and day trips waking up at 4am to get on the road weren't uncommon. Hansel's car once broke down during a group trip in Tahoe, and we "had to" stay at Caesar's Palace until the car was fixed. This was way before Zoom; we probably didn't even have the internet on our laptops. We probably didn't even *have* laptops – the easy life, back in the day. Everyone else went home first, but Wayne stuck around. What can you do if you're stuck in Tahoe but snowboard and gamble for three days straight? Not a bad way to find a best friend.

Sometime after that, we had a random lunch at Hansel's uncle's house, when his Popo (grandma) from Hong Kong was visiting.

She spoke very broken English, probably not even enough to communicate with Wayne. After Wayne left, Popo turned to Hansel with a smile on her face and softly said "Nei hai mm hai… gay?" She said it with a smirk as if to give some extra context, implying, "Not that there's anything wrong with that." It took a few seconds for Hansel to realize that the last word, "gay," wasn't Cantonese, but English – and that Popo was asking him "Are you gay?" When an old Chinese grandma mistakes your brotherly love for gay love, it lands somewhere between awkwardness and embarrassment, but that's when you know you might be best friends.

We even went heli-boarding, James Bond style. Everything suddenly drops to slow-mo, and above the din of the thwup-thwup-thwup, we share a look as we strap on our boards, jump from the helicopter, and high-five just before we land on that sweet, sweet powder. Or, did we pay a lot of money to get a 2-hour safety talk and to be carefully escorted away from the spinning blades of death onto a hillside with a little more snow than a normal trail? I guess it depends on who we're telling the story to. Back then, it was James Bond and cliff jumps. Now, it's Wayne who got stuck 5 feet after he started, and there was barely any snow for all that money, effort, and heli-gas, otherwise known as the truth. But we were young, single, flush with cash, and trying random stuff out for the story to tell. Little did we know that was the start of spending up for the badass experiences (well, after a 20-year delay or so).

Asian Yuppies

There was a lot of consulting work in the Bay Area, the place where everyone with any technical skill was moving to in the late 90's. The Bay Area was already overrun with Asians, and still more would come to cash in on the tech gold rush of the day, including us. We grew up seeing Alex P. Keaton on *Family Ties* and Gordon Gecko in *Wall Street* – that's how we saw money. You didn't have to like Gordon Gecko (although some of our investment banker friends *loved* him) to want to be able to afford everything you ever wanted. And you didn't have to be white either, based on all the successful Asians we met during the Silicon Valley boom.

The friends we met in the late 90's in Silicon Valley were smart as crap. Every other one of our friends was Asian, from a top school, and had a great job. Vicki and Jim went to Brown. Dave and Emmet graduated from UPenn. Rich and Telly went to Harvard Business School, and then you had Alan, Tina, Lisa, Linda, Al, Jeff, Bayle, and a buttload of others from Stanford. Not that the school you went to years ago *really* matters. We even had a couple of "I went to a school in Boston" humble-braggers. AIYA!!! If you went to Harvard, just *say* you went to Harvard, you douchebag. They were investment bankers, directors of development teams, hedge-fund managers, or doctors. It's like the Asian tiger parents all got together and decided to put all their kids in one place.

The Bay Area during the dot-com boom was like a magnet for smart, successful, Asians – and we were there to try to get a piece of it. For us, with WashU ranked "only" about 15th in the country back then, we were clearly inferior. That is the very definition of first-world problems, right?

Asian Parties

If you'd have caught Wayne in 1995, you'd find him trying to learn to surf and play beach volleyball. He hadn't yet hung out with any Asians, and he was certainly never going to date one. Until he met Hansel in 1997 and was introduced to the fabled Asian parties, Wayne was a full-on banana. Or a ball of rice rolled in piss – yellow outside, white inside.

Wayne had never even thought of going to an Asian party. Back in Alabama, debutantes would have their "coming-out parties" to introduce young women into society. Wayne was getting ready to have his coming-out party to introduce himself to the Asian scene. "Hello World, I'm coming out of the racial closet. I'm Asian, and I'm proud, dammit."

"How cool can Asian parties be?" Wayne remembers thinking at first. "Everyone's going to have an accent, everyone's going to be dorky..." Like we said, we can be a bit racist. Hansel, on the other hand, was racist the other way – Asian or nothing for him. White people suck. And now, he was about to break it all wide open for Wayne. And being in the San Francisco area meant Asians were damn near everywhere, especially when they were gathered with their own kind at a dance party.

M Society West and Element were two groups that made a killing on these kinds of parties. Somewhere, there's an email list of all the Asian people who would pay a $20 cover charge every other weekend or so to go to these things. That was a good chunk of change back then and a good chunk now, inflation be damned. But the Asian yuppies were down. Where else would you meet other hot Asians with money but at one of these club parties? These were all the same Asians, too – young with good jobs, good money, and good-looking.

An Asian New Years party with token white guy Mike Bayle. We're in the middle, in case we all look the same to you.

With the bass absolutely ripping your ears to shreds and lights doing much the same to your eyeballs, if you were lucky enough to walk in there today, you'd be struck by the fashion choices at least. All the girls were in slim-fitting black, showing a lot more skin than you'd like if one of them was your daughter. All the guys were in a white ribbed t-shirt, a black necklace, and a medium-length black leather coat from J. Crew. We both had all of it, and thought we were cool as shit, even if we did look like every other Asian dude. Looking back, we're very aware of how we looked… like absolute idiots. But make no mistake, back then we looked hot as hell, and you can't tell us otherwise.

1998 -2000

1998 in San Francisco was so fun for us that we coined it our Summer of '98. Doesn't have the same ring as Summer of '69, but Bryan Adams summed it up well – we wouldn't be standing on our mama's porch, but those were some of the best days of our lives. We were in our late 20's and going out every weekend, with no idea that we were on the verge of finding girlfriends and wives and life-long friends. Going into business together would have been a reach for us at that stage – we weren't experienced enough, nor were we mentally (or financially) ready just yet. But we were pumping life into every single moment we could, living in the middle of the San Francisco Asian scene during a huge tech boom.

We often hung out with our buddy Dave, the third leg of our friendship tripod. He's a bigger dude and a real goofball, and when he'd had a few drinks, he became the funniest guy you've ever met. That's why we called him Fun Dave, like Fun Bobby from *Friends*, because for those 20 minutes when he had a buzz going, he was the life of the party. Of course, once that buzz was gone, he'd be whining about every girl he met. These days, we have an annual dinner at Sizzler, a special occasion, so we go one step above White Castle. We don't hang like we used to, but Dave will always be that third dude we would have brought into theCoderSchool next.

That summer, Hansel had that proverbial rich uncle who lent him a place to stay right in the middle of the financial district, close to Chinatown and near the red-light district of San Francisco. To give you an idea of how rich this uncle is: his current San Francisco home is in an exclusive gated community, home to senators and billionaires' children. The neighborhood is so prestigious, there's even a book about its historical houses. "Hansel's Place" was the kind of place you'd walk into and ask what Hansel did for a living. "I have a rich-uncle, that's how I roll" was the party-line answer. Many a pre-party gathering was had here, and many a full-on party too (sorry, Uncle Tim).

The only hangover cure we ever needed was New Sun Hong Kong on Broadway, which, thankfully, didn't close until 4 AM. We'd arrive at 2:30 in the morning and close the place down with orders of wonton mein, Singapore noodles, and maybe even a little greasy duck, all ordered in Cantonese by Hansel, of course. Sometimes, it was just us and Fun Dave, and other times, we brought a whole group of women to impress. Late-night duck head is impressive indeed. If we were still together the next morning, that's when we'd get jook, a Hong Kong rice porridge, at Hing Lung. Jook was our original White Castle – that cheap as hell stuff that's greasy and might give you the runs. And you'd crave it, too, just like those steamed sliders with cheese. It was yet another introduction into the Asian scene for Wayne, who was more used to a bowl full of grits.

Every weekend was like a house party from every 80s movie you've ever seen. Only Mom and Dad weren't coming back, and everyone was yellow. By the time New Year's Eve 1999 rolled around, everyone was ready for the ultimate party, so Hansel and his soon-to-be-wife Lisa delivered with their own personal black-tie gala at the uncle's place. The place was packed to the rafters, with live music by Hansel and Fun Dave's new band SPAM. Short for Spam Fried Rice and just as terrible, they started light with the Scooby Doo theme song and ended heavy with some *Marvin Gaye* and *Let's Get It On*. That was Hansel's first hint that a band can't suck when the entire audience is drunk. We were popping bubbly, dancing up on each other (well, maybe not *each-other* each-other, and not that there'd be anything wrong with that) and blowing the roof off with our music. A room filled with coders, bankers, doctors, and venture capitalists, all maybe slightly curious whether this Y2K bug would blow up the entire world.

Fortunately for everyone, as day broke and we got some jook in our bellies, the hangovers went away, and nobody died. Best of all, Y2K wasn't really anything. We were safe. Unless you count the impending doom of a stock market bubble on the verge of bursting that we all wish we'd seen coming. It wasn't the end of the fun, though. Not for us and Asian parties. Not for us as friends. Not even for Hansel as a lead singer. This was only the beginning. We were about to live through our own personal Spinal Tap moment. Soon, we'd be turning it up to eleven... with Timmy Ramen.

Chapter 4

The Rockstar Bros

We might call ourselves theCoderBros, but for a brief period in the early aughts, we had our rockstar period. Maybe "star" is overstating it a bit, or maybe it's not, but that's absolutely how it felt at the time. Music – even though neither of us is very musical – was weirdly a kind of salvation for the two of us. It all started with SPAM, the Y2K band that Hansel and Fun Dave put together with their friend Gin. And while it started on the high of the turn of the millennium, we started to thrive when things got bad for the tech world we lived in, when the stock and job markets crashed.

In the early 2000s, both of us and pretty much all of our friends lost their jobs right around the same time, like most of Silicon Valley. All of the San Francisco Bay Area had a little bit of "The world is going to hell in a handbasket" kind of feeling. It's kind of like how everyone felt at the beginning of the pandemic. Only instead of getting a COVID puppy or having meetings through Zoom, we had SPAM. The band, that is. SPAM and its success at the Y2K party were definitely ongoing topics at that time, as was meeting women. During one of these typical conversations at one of those crazy Asian parties, Wayne drunkenly slurred to Hansel,

"Dude, I need to be in the band!"

"What do you play?" Hansel yelled over the room.

"Nothin'!"

"Sweet!" Hansel smiled. "You're in!"

Just like that, Wayne was in the mix. Through our love of Timmy from *South Park* and ramen and being Chinese (yeah, we know, ramen's Japanese - but close enough), the band's name changed, and Timmy Ramen was born. Definitely a choir singing "Hallelujah" kind of moment. As Timmy Ramen, we kicked our fair share of ass onstage as an all-Asian cover band. Our M.O. was to get drunk, play our favorite songs and light the room on fire. For our first few months of practice, we took advantage of the tech downturn and used the empty space at the startup that Hansel worked at, Mobilocity. Picture a big loft with multiple offices that could probably fit 50, but at the time, only had 3. Instead of using the conference room to close huge deals, there was a drum set, amps, and mics.

Timmaaaaaaaah!

For gigs, we started out doing the thing that real artists would never do. The first bar we played at only let us play because we paid them $200. This is not normally the recipe for success. Fortunately, this was a drop in the bucket for what we figured would be our first and only show. We'd be a legend throughout the Bay Area as that one Asian band that rocked the joint and was never heard from again.

Seriously, the odds of us playing again were statistically very low – we were bound to flop, mostly because the band was just not that good. We were a karaoke band that played covers, and Hansel's karaoke was only one level above William Hung of *American Idol* fame. But we had an ace up our sleeves – we were consultants, and damn if we weren't going to consult our way through this like some business project.

Timmy Ramen groupies who we're still friends with, including Hansel's wife Lisa in the cowboy hat

We invited our huge group of Asian friends (and, of course, a couple of token white guys) and basically said to come out to this bar we rented to watch us be idiots on stage. We packed the house that night and instead of a rock show, it was like we'd launched a new social scene/business model. We had a cute guest singer named Leilani, we had an onstage birthday celebration, and we sped up the songs to be faster to sound like punk-pop covers. It was consulting 101 – put lipstick on a pig and get those customers what they wanted. In this case, they wanted fun, and we had that in spades. Sure, there were other large-scale Asian parties, most of them hosted by Element, but ours had the twist of going to a rock concert as well. We sold so many drinks that bars loved us – not because we were good, but because we had an awesome model. Who cares about quality of music if drinks are being sold, right?

Unless you're crazy talented, it ain't easy to build a following with a cover band. We didn't have the talent – but we had a gimmick. Our gimmick was five Asian dudes (and one hot Asian girl) playing in a rock band. And we'd all scream "Timmaaaaaah! Jaba-jaba-ja!" just like the South Park guy in the wheelchair while doing the rock 'n roll devil horns with our fingers. Musically, we sucked, and listening back on it, sure, it was a little cringy. Okay, maybe even a lot cringy. But we had all our drunk friends singing along to songs we knew they knew. We knew our audience – because they were just like us – and that's all a successful act really needs. And a little bit of alcohol never hurts either.

To get deeper into the karaoke comparison, everyone in the audience was there to sing, too. They'd sing along with our repertoire of hits like "Fight for Your Right (To Party)," "Jack and Diane," "Brown Eyed Girl," and "Sweet Caroline," complete with all the "bum-bum-bum" and "so good, so good" that gets the blood flowing. That Blink-182 punk-pop style sound was in vogue then, so we'd turn all our songs into an upbeat bar-chord frenzy and simplify the song whenever we could. Which is to say, as long as every song only had about four chords, we were good to go. We were a marketing gimmick, but a successful one.

The Group

The band's core was the tripod – us two and Fun Dave. Hansel was the lead karaoke singer because he was still the best singer in the group, and that's not saying much. All his childhood piano lessons helped, as he later picked up guitar and drumming on his own – though he still can't read a lick of music. As for Wayne, he had never played an instrument in his life, not even the Chinese standard of violin or piano growing up. But he was "backup guitar" whatever that is, and all he had to do was strap on a guitar, turn his amp to zero, and look good. We're still not sure if he's yet played an instrument in his life.

Fun Dave was our bassist, having of course never played the bass before joining the band. Dave was originally a friend of Haniel's (Hansel's brother) from UPenn but ended up hanging out more with us when he moved to San Francisco from Philly. He was a quick study, too, and even without a musical background could knock out the base riff from Michael Jackson's "Billy Jean" and get the audience pumped.

Then there was Telly, our lead guitarist. He's a graduate of Rice University and has an MBA from Harvard. Not the kind of guy you'd typically associate with a rock band, except that, without a doubt, Telly was our only *real* musician. He is a legit heavy-metal guitarist, and even looked the part with his super long hair at that time, so he naturally became our lead guitar. If you ever hear him dive into Ozzy's "Crazy Train," you'll know we made the right choice.

Timmy Ramen (left to right)
Dave, Hansel, Wayne, random drummer,
Telly. Random girl?

The real unpredictable part – just like in *This is Spinal Tap* – was our drummer. If you don't remember, in that movie, their drummers keep getting replaced because they keep dying off. One spontaneously combusts onstage. That never happened to any of ours; although come to think of it, what a marketing gimmick that would have been. In our case, we just couldn't nail down the right guy. We once tried to get one off of Craigslist – we put an ad out specifically looking for an Asian drummer, and someone genuinely responded to that ad and called us racist. Wait, if we *want* an Asian, is that racist? Or is it affirmative action?

Our first drummer was Gin, now a cryptocurrency guy. It was he and Hansel, over a bowl of wonton noodles, that decided to start the band back in late 1999. He had too much going on though and was eventually replaced by Scott. Scott was this really nice guy we met through Telly – he was a classic Silicon Valley tech guy who played *way* too fast. When Wayne sang The Ramones' "I Wanna Be Sedated," Scott's drumming was anything but. It was like he drank 10 espressos – by the end Wayne was singing like an auctioneer on speed with 20, 20, 24 hours to go. We slowed things down with Joe Cha, a startup CEO by day. He had this clean-cut MBA look, which wasn't why he left, but he did. Then there was Frank, who played in socks even at the gigs with the gross beer-stained floors. Ed was in there somewhere, a good drummer in keeping time, but he could never get the intro to "All the Small Things" right. At the end, there was Cole, who had a screamin' awesome voice, too, and was a *real* musician unlike most of us.

The whole experience was a trip, to be honest. We started getting paid a little bit to perform – enough to get us a few drinks at the end of the night. We played hard and we brought the rock-show experience, honestly pretty impressive for a cover band that was terrible.

One night – Wayne's first night – we went so hard that Wayne fell off the stage with a loud KA-THUMP! The guitars screeched to a halt and the drums quit pounding and the audience went deadly silent. In a cheesy comedy, this is where you'd hear a record scratch. Two seconds later, Wayne threw up his hands, Fun Dave yelped into the mic "He's okay!!," and the audience just screamed, "YEEAAHHH!!" Then we were immediately back at it, picking up right where we left off.

For what was basically our first joint business venture, we were hitting it out of the park, and proving that we get knocked down, but then get up again. You were, as the song says, never going to keep us down. Especially not with our secret weapon.

The Flavor Packet

Timmy Ramen may have been our thing, but that "thing" had a lot of sausage, and we only had so many friends to invite. We needed to figure out how to constantly get new people, preferably hot new people, i.e., hot new women. The secret weapon? Let's find hot girls outside our friend group to be a guest singer for a few songs - a different hot girl for every gig. We swear, if we could have sold stock in that, it'd be a unicorn business by now. We'd find a random hot Asian chick, ask them if they wanted to sing in our band (regardless of if they could actually sing) and find some stuff roughly within their range. Suddenly, it was even less on our shoulders to get people in the room. The Flavor Packet would bring their lady friends, and that would pack the joint with more hot women dressed in rocker outfits – a sexier version of the Asian club outfits. And what better name for a rotating spicy-hot guest singer than the Flavor Packet, instant ramen's best friend.

It's amazing what the promise of a single night of "fame" will convince the girls to put up with. No, we never hooked up with them, although looking back it sure sounds like the perfect setup.

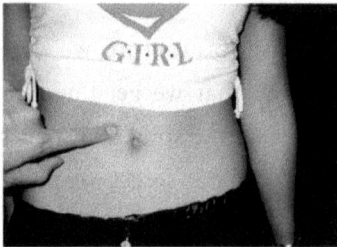

Connie's Abs

The closest we came was poking Connie's washboard abs all night because, you know, rocker outfit. She's probably still our favorite Flavor Packet with those abs. Or maybe it was Leilani, who rotated in most often and we were closest friends with and was super cool. We never poked her abs though - didn't want to get knocked out by the boyfriend Al, who was a literal Army Ranger. Nicole, Jennifer, Jin, Aileen, Cindy, Jenn, Cocaine Girl, and even Henry (our only dude packet who then started another band called Tiger Bomb) also joined in the fun as Flavor Packets at some point. Sorry to any we might have missed – it was honestly a bit of a whirlwind. Cocaine Girl, if you're reading this, be sure to remind us what your name was.

The Flavor Packet's name, and sometimes picture, would go out in our invites to our friends, who were always looking for something new (gotta please the customers, right?). Who doesn't want to come check out a new spicy flavor? For her friends, of course, it's their first time seeing their flavor friend sing, so it was a way of reliably reliving that first, amazing time onstage for the Packet. With our skills recreating a first success by just changing how the package looks, it's frankly shocking neither of us were ever recruited to be in Apple's marketing department. In Yoda's voice "Think Different, and Different Thinking We Did." We're usually very humble folk, but let's be honest here, the Flavor Packet was pure genius.

We didn't look at this whole thing like a real business – even while things were going nuts in our work lives, this was an escape. We were playing fun songs to psyched audiences, fronted by a sexy lady who wanted to dress the part. Hansel even started getting recognized as the lead singer of a band, which is a bit of a crazy rock-star moment. At one of the Asian parties, he went to pay the cover, but the guy taking tickets let him go on through for free. "I came up from LA one time and saw one of your gigs! You're the lead singer, right? Timmy Ramen rocks!" And rock we did, we even had dorky business cards with the band's tagline - "Timmy. Because we rock."

The whole Asian rock band scene started to catch on. You can't franchise a band, but people can copy you. Other Asians saw us onstage and thought, "if they can do it, we can, too!" We were an attainable level of talent and success, and that can move mountains. The dumber and easier it is to attain, the more copycats you'll get. Bands like Tiger Bomb, PLA, Buda Belly, and Funk U were all our Asian friends forming new bands and having similarly awesome party gigs. Nothing more flattering than imitation, right? Sometimes it was even more fun yelling from the audience, especially because you can drink a lot more being in the audience than being in the band. Hell, Hansel even played drums in a separate Asian band called Green Chink 182 (a Green Day and Blink 182 cover group). If you think that band name was racist, you should see the tees we designed for our short-lived but hilariously racist company, Cheeky Chink. Definitely more on this later.

Bimbo's

The culmination of all our work with Timmy Ramen happened at a venue that had seen the likes of The Stooges, and Marvin Gaye, even Dennis Quaid. Yes, Dennis Quaid had a band, and they played there just a few days before Timmy Ramen. This was a huge, historical club called Bimbo's 365. One of the biggest San Francisco cover bands in the day, Tainted Love, was looking for an opener and found us and reached out. To put that in perspective, that's about as random-awesome as when Neil Patrick Harris showed up looking for p*ssy in *Harold and Kumar*. Keep in mind that not long before this we'd paid $200 to a bar to play a bunch of covers, and now we had people hauling our equipment and setting it up for us. We even had our band name up in the big marquee sign out in front. Seeing our band name up in lights was a sign of the awesome things to come that night.

Dave, Telly, Hansel, Drummer Ed, Wayne

The days of pay-to-play were in the rearview, and now we had experienced audio engineers doing a sound check for us. Maybe a leap too far, based on our complete lack of experience. The lead sound guy asks Hansel if he wants a boom mic and he shrugs, having no idea what a boom mic is. We were total rookies, but somehow playing the biggest stage. Then they point us toward the green room. Wayne's reaction summed up our inexperience: 'What's a green room?' In ours, there were Coronas because they'd asked us what kind of beer we liked ahead of time. We just thought they were being friendly when they asked but turns out rock-star status also gives you choice of beer. So we cracked a few, some of us fidgeting nervously to be out on a big stage, and waited for the arrival of Karsten Lemm.

Karsten Lemm was a German journalist visiting the US specifically to cover what Silicon Valley tech bros were doing on their "off time," a.k.a. the time their severance (if they had any left) was paying for. Word of this new music scene – including the niche we'd inadvertently created – had gotten to him in Germany, so he was here to write something up for *Stern*, Germany's most widely-read magazine. Write something about _us_? He wanted to interview _us_ for the biggest magazine in Germany? Screw that we didn't understand a lick of German, we were stoked that a journalist had traveled from Germany to cover us - all because Hansel and his buddy Gin had spontaneously decided to start a band. This made no sense, and we loved it.

That night was beyond memorable. The stage was huge – bigger than anything we'd ever stood on – and the house was packed. Only this time it wasn't just our Asian friends. It was a mix of people there to see us and to see Tainted Love, the hugely popular 80's cover band that we were opening for, that catered to a lot of the white yuppies that lived in the Marina area of San Francisco. It was a brand-new crowd for us, and we won them over.

We played "All the Small Things," and one of the white guys later told us we played it better than Blink 182. We'll take that, even if it was an exaggeration. We busted out Jimmy Eat World's "The Middle", and the entire band (and some of the audience) jumped in sync to the chorus – K-pop bands, eat your hearts out. Telly got to show his chops playing the solo to

"Crazy Train" for the first time; if only he played it with his teeth and on his back, we could have gotten him on MTV. We debuted our version of "Sweet Caroline", but of course our punk-pop fast-and-loud version. "Touching me, touching you", became Hansel grabbing his crotch and then pointing to a girl named Caroline. Not sure what he was thinking, that could be a sexual harassment lawsuit these days.

The highlight of the night had to be our rendition of "In the End", a Linkin Park song. We had the whole audience in sync with us while Wayne blew them away with all the rap verses. Wayne, seeing he's got the audience in the palm of his hands, starts screaming, "Here we go! Here we go, everybody!!" just as Hansel starts into the chorus, and the whole crowd, probably 300 deep, takes the cue and goes nuts. Then Hansel takes that energy and starts moshing with the band onstage – while still singing – bringing yet another level of energy. It was a moment – it was THE moment. When you have hundreds of people jumping up and down in sync and singing along with you like you're the next Kurt Cobain, it's something you remember for the rest of your life. Maximum rockstar moment, shared with your BFF. We were on top of the world that night, and it wasn't lost on us that we'd fallen ass-backwards into the whole thing. This is a theme that would continue through to theCoderSchool.

Rockstar Moments Are Forever

Bimbo's 365 might have been the peak, but it was far from the end for Timmy Ramen. We were now playing all different types of venues, mixing up the set list, even working up some parodies. We changed "What's My Age Again" to "Who's Your Asian Friend?" which worked out perfectly when we ended up playing at an Element Asian party, a scene that had launched our whole friendship. Some hot girl even took off her bra and threw it at Hansel onstage, mid-set. Whatever you've heard about rock bands and being the star of the show, it's true (but divide it by 100 for us).

The rockin' Asian audience from the stage POV

When we played at the Element party, we ended our set just before the space turned into a dance club to 400 Asians, all of whom seemed to want to high five us as we came off stage. Steve Chen, the party producer, walked over to us with champagne in one hand and a wad of cash in the other, fighting the crowd to get to us. He handed us the bottle and the cash and just said, "you guys killed it!" If there's one guy who knows what a crowd likes, it's Steve. When someone is fighting through a crowd to hand you a wad of cash and champagne, that's what you call a rockstar moment.

Rockstar Moments Aren't Actually Forever

We knew this wouldn't last, so we didn't take it for granted while we had it. If Timmy Ramen ever does a reunion show we probably won't be doing shots before and after like we were doing back then, but we'd still have that same feeling, just enjoying what life gives us. To quote Karsten Lemm, in *Stern*, "It was the center of the new economy. Now everyone in California's Silicon Valley is waiting for the next boom - and enjoying life in the meantime."

Timmy Ramen lasted about three years, with Wayne dropping out first, and Hansel playing for another year or two before he had kids, when the band petered out. There was one gig when Hansel's wife Lisa was pregnant and sitting in the back, when Hansel wondered if the loud music would hurt the baby. Baby Maile turned out all right, but that was the beginning of the end.

We realized we were way out of our element and probably never should have been there, but for us to get a peek at the life of a real rock star, doing it the way we did was pretty special. We peaked early and lasted well after Bimbo's, but we never quite got back to that level. We do still have the equipment though, and Hansel occasionally still picks up his guitar and plays. Nowadays, though, it's much more likely that we'll go to cheer on Beck, Hansel's son, who's now in his own Asian band. The apple doesn't fall far from the tree, so rock on, young grasshopper.

Chapter 5

Failed Horses

In business terminology, a unicorn is a privately-owned startup business worth over a billion dollars. Think OpenAI, SpaceX, or Uber (back before it became public). Get investors, spend like mad, then swing for the fences and get big or die trying. Remember Quibi? They died trying. Webvan? Pets.com? There are tons of them. Of course, if you've gotten this far in the book and thought we were about to tell you the secret to creating a billion-dollar company, catch us in the next book. But if you're interested in a business that means something to you, something more than money, maybe we can give you some tips. It's called a "lifestyle business," and in Silicon Valley, that's a four-letter word. But those four letters fit us just fine.

A lifestyle business is one that has low startup costs and minimal overhead that actually makes a profit, enough for a certain lifestyle – hence the name. It isn't as rare or hard to build as a unicorn – it's just… a normal horse. Even so, it can take a while to get there, and if you're an idea machine like Hansel or a hard worker like Wayne, you're probably going to start a lot of businesses that don't do as well as you'd hoped. It also isn't easy, which is why before theCoderSchool, we failed a lot. Sometimes together, sometimes

apart, but we failed, nonetheless. Enough times to make up a whole chapter.

CRAP

The first failed idea ironically is our longest lived and is still being used today. The Cost Reimbursement Allocation Program, or CRAP, was ahead of its time in functionality and naming convention. The idea and name originated from our 3rd amigo, Fun Dave. It was basically just a spreadsheet to help groups of people figure out who pays for what after a group trip. Say you're going on a ski trip to Tahoe with a bunch of friends – you pay for the hotel, she pays for the ski tickets, and they pay for gas. How do you split it afterwards? This was the 90's, people, we were literally writing "I owe Wayne $100" on a napkin – until we could CRAP it.

It wasn't so much the tool itself that was awesome. It was that it made it SO much easier to do a trip with friends – there was no more fuss about splitting the dinner or the groceries. One person pays, then it goes to CRAP, and we deal with money at the end. That's one lesson to learn from CRAP – when a tool actually changes behavior, those are the ones that stick.

CRAP never really became a business as much as just a cool tool. All of our friends used it, and our wives both still do. The best part was whenever someone paid for something, we'd all be like "Just CRAP it!" Fun to say, fun to use. Nowadays there are plenty of apps like this, and even Venmo has something like it. But there's nothing like a good old-fashioned spreadsheet with a killer catchphrase. CRAP IT!

Fantasy TeeVee (FTV)

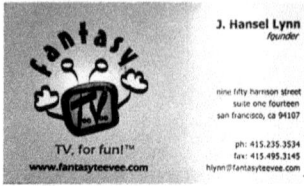

An FTV business card

We both love sports, and we've both played fantasy football for a long time. We also watched a ton of TV, so it's not a surprise what came next. Instead of taking a fantasy football game and coding our own version of it, we juked left and created a non-sports variation on the same idea – Fantasy TV. If fantasy football could charge a football fan a few bucks to play, why couldn't we do the same for the TV fans out there?

Instead of a quarterback scoring points with touchdowns, it was Kramer scoring points by busting in the door, or Rachel getting a bonus by kissing Phoebe (remember that episode?!). That was FantasyTeevee.com in a nutshell. Bear in mind, this was during the early days of cable TV, when Netflix was still a DVD-by-mail service with those red envelopes. It was a pretty small subset of shows, so it was a lot easier for everyone to find and watch the same shows at the same time because the channels you had were the channels you had.

There was a lot of work on our part to make Fantasy TeeVee function at all, of course. Other than theCoderSchool, this was our closest attempt at a "real" company together. Business cards, a fully built custom website, partnerships with other companies – but no investors (not that anyone would invest). It was just the two of us, and we would split the coding work and just go for it, like any startup. It was a full-time, unpaid job while we built that website, hoping to turn that into money at some point. Our desks were littered with red bull cans and empty Cheeto bags, just like in the movies.

At that time, automating the point scoring wasn't feasible because the data wasn't there. We had to literally watch stuff on *Tivo*, and manually keep track of characters, whether someone said a name, how many minutes onscreen, if someone kissed…. All in a notebook. Imagine watching TV with your wife with a notebook, and you're both like "WAIT! He came onscreen, start the watch!" "Hold on, did that count as a kiss?!" Not the most scalable business model. Every night, we'd tally up the scores and enter them into our newly built custom website, so our players could see how many points they got in their matchup.

Playing Fantasy TeeVee was free to begin with, but eventually we decided to start charging $10 per game because keeping all these details straight was a time-consuming pain in the ass and because we had to try to make money somehow. At one point, we had over 15,000 users in our database, which is still amazing to us. But of course, as soon as we started charging, that number became about 2. That's when we knew we had to look for real jobs. Towards the end, we found one player named Terry Free – awesome, awesome dude. He LOVED the game and the concept and volunteered to help us track everything, for free. Wherever you are Terry, we appreciate the heck out of you and will split our company earnings with you 50/50! What's your address so we can mail you the $5??

We even partnered with a few legit companies at the height of Fantasy TeeVee. Zap2it, who was eventually bought by TV Guide, put a co-branded version of FTV on their website, right along with their TV listings. Yes, there was a time when you would go on the internet to see what was on TV. We even got in the door to pitch a partnership at Yahoo! which was bigger than Google back then, but they basically laughed us out the door.

It felt like a long time, but we were probably going at it unpaid for a little under a year. Wayne first ran out of money and decided to get a job, then Hansel followed shortly after and FTV was put on life support. The company was a total flop, money-wise, but not in terms of traffic and usage, or the lessons learned. The main lesson: free is way, way different than paid. In hindsight, maybe that's pretty obvious.

iPhone Apps

How do you learn to build an app? By building an app. Fifteen years before founding theCoderSchool, Hansel applied what would become its core philosophy – learning by doing. He taught himself to build iPhone apps by just tinkering with it until he figured it out.

His first app, the Hot-o-meter, was perfect for our Asian clubbing days. It turned your iPhone 4, or whatever low number it was back then, into something that looked like a Geiger counter. When you pointed it towards a hot girl, it started beeping off the charts, and when you turned it toward a dork, it'd just flatline and buzz. Of course, there wasn't any code to detect a hot girl – instead it just worked on a compass. Point it north and it's hot, point it south and it's cold. You just had to pull out the smooth playa moves to pull one over on the ladies – and make sure you pointed in the right direction. Genius.

Something more useful was Mogo Photo. If you need the perfect photo but don't have perfect timing, you probably now rely on the Live Photos feature of an iPhone. Take a bunch of photos so you can choose the best one. Hansel created this exact thing before it came by default with the iPhone. This was back in the day when the Fart App made about $10,000 a day, so let's just say competition wasn't fierce. Basically, he used the video camera function and programmed an app that turned video frames effectively into live photos.

When Bloomberg Business Week did an article on apps early on, it featured Hansel's app. It was a stunning success, netting him about ten bucks. Of course, Apple went and took the idea for themselves and made it a default part of the phone. We're certain Steve Jobs found the app on his App Store and said, "this is brilliant!" Relatively certain. Lesson learned? Technology moves ridiculously fast – solving for a technical problem is best left for the big boys and unicorns – not the lifestyle businesses.

Peepee Pants

We begin this failure with a poop story. Hansel is a triathlete and did an Ironman in Sacramento years ago. After making the massive mistake of carbo-loading on a fully loaded burrito from Chipotle, beans and all, he started driving to his race.

Picture Hansel driving by himself in his Toyota Sienna minivan, with his bike in the back and a snack bag in the passenger seat. Friday afternoon traffic is ridiculous, so he was stuck in traffic on the San Francisco Bay Bridge when suddenly the need struck as soon as he got on the bridge. Like REALLY struck, with no exit ramp anywhere close because of the traffic. He looked around the car in desperation, his eyes settling on an Asian classic.

"Should I just... empty that instant ramen bowl and take a dump in it?" he said to himself. Now, this was the Korean kind, where the bowl is about 5" in diameter. At least it wasn't Cup o' Noodles, so he had a shot. While that would have been an amazing story, he just didn't have the dexterity to pull it off. Instead, he ended up crapping his pants in the car and heading into an Old Navy 20 minutes later and limping slowly to the bathroom (you know, so it doesn't fall out).

After Wayne heard this story – and laughed his ass off – the idea of Peepee Pants was born. He's had to help parents who are at that age – in a home, needing diapers, etc. – and now was naturally concerned that his BFF had been in dire need of effluent-protectant garments even though he's still sharp as a tack. No adult ought to be ashamed of needing them, but nobody likes how those things look. Why not invent a stylish pant with diapers built in? These wouldn't necessarily be Poopoo Pants, but at least first-gen Peepee Pants. Astronaut-level design, but with a good fit and a fashionable look.

They're not just for senior citizens or people post-surgery. We wouldn't have to leave a sporting event where we can't get up. Can you imagine the Super Bowl commercial we would run:

Dude 1: What are you doin'?

Dude 2: I'm peein' RIGHT NOW! (With a big smile)

Peepee Pants didn't get off the ground like so many ideas, but we still don't hate it. Give us a few, and maybe this high fashion pant is how we get to the Met Gala. As for the lesson learned? Ask any shark on Shark Tank – an idea is worth exactly zero dollars – it's the execution that counts. Perhaps a more important lesson, however, is to always buy instant ramen bowls with at least an 8-inch diameter.

Cheeky Chink Tees

We can say the name of the company, but you probably shouldn't. Our logo was a guy with a rice hat, slanty eyes, and a bowl cut, just like Wayne when he was a kid. Cheeky Chink Tees offered offensive t-shirts

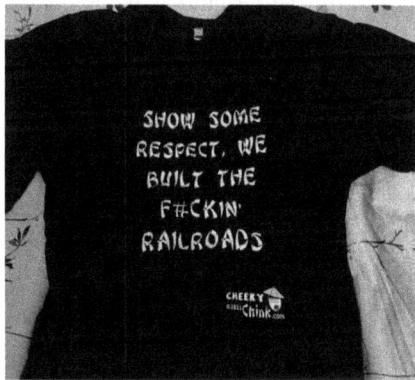
Our Classic Tee

in line with the offensive name. Our most famous (to us, anyway) t-shirt creation said, "Show Some Respect, We Built the F#ckin Railroads." We were always wanting to get some famous Asian stars to wear it and spread the word. John Cho, we're still down, even though you're Korean. As the original White Castle dude, you can definitely be an honorary Chinese. Sure, you built the fuckin' railroads.

Some of our other classics were a smiley white face amongst a grid of smiley yellow faces for "Token White Guy" or "Flower Bridge", which when translated to Cantonese sounds like Faaaahk Yoo. Try having your grandma from Hong Kong translate *that* for you.

Then there was the "Be Like Water" shirt, one of Bruce Lee's core philosophies (did you know he was a philosopher?). Not offensive in and of itself, just a nod to the Man himself. Basically, it means don't be trapped in one mindset, be flexible and adapt to change – like water. Pretty high-minded for a t-shirt company that was us being as racist as we could be. We'll go one further and say that to Be Water is to also never stand still – always keep moving, keep improving, keep building on yourself. The journey never stops.

Cudos

During the pandemic, Hansel and his wife Lisa felt a lot of pent-up business energy. theCoderSchool was already thriving at the time, but Lisa had an itch and Hansel thought he had time to help her run it. They had a great plan for a frozen custard and donut shop called Cudos (custard + donuts, get it?), bought the equipment and the stock and everything, and even rented a prime spot. It would have been a prime model to franchise, just like theCoderSchool.

A cup o' Cudos

For those of you not from the Midwest, frozen custard is like ice cream, but thicker, smoother, and richer with egg yolk added in. In the Midwest, lines form around the block for frozen custard, but it wasn't something known yet in the West. Despite using his own advice about reusing a working model (and having a cool memorable name), it didn't take off and was closed after a year and a half. Mad respect to all food-related businesses out there, it's tough stuff. Hansel ended up installing that giant commercial custard-making machine in his garage, and still eats that frozen custard daily.

In the end, Hansel and Lisa were lucky to have gotten out basically unscathed, save losing only about $25,000 in total and a heck of a lot of effort. The lease was entirely taken over by a new business, which isn't common, but allowed them to get out of the 5-year lease entirely. Hansel and Lisa's biggest win was putting their middle and high school kids to work for some great job experience, something every kid should have. The second biggest win is having a commercial quality frozen custard maker in their garage, with soooooo much custard leftover. Despite all the headaches, money, and effort they spent, there was never a regret for taking a shot. After all, you make 0% of the shots you don't take.

Part 2

Rold and Kumar Get Hungry

Chapter 6

The Idea

✦————————✦

After a chapter-full of wrong ideas, we're finally hitting on the right idea – theCoderSchool. It is, of course, why we call ourselves theCoderBros. And it is, for as long as we can keep it going, what we live and breathe, and why we wrote this book. As with any good idea, there's an origin story – and this is ours.

At first, Hansel wasn't even looking to become an entrepreneur. He was just desperate to get out of the corporate world because at the ripe old age of 40, he finally realized that the world of big-tech and corporate grind was just not his cup of tea. He wanted to control his life, be his own boss, and focus on his family and young kids.

He and Lisa had been flipping houses since the late 2000s' flipping craze, and after he quit his corporate tech job (circa 2010), that became his full-time gig. Until he realized that real estate development involves a lot of downtime waiting for permits or construction. Hansel needed something to satisfy that pent-up desire to build, to create, to do something with his mind – something like… a magazine subscription.

Hansel had been living the house-flipping life for about a year when he noticed an ad for the School of Rock in his latest issue of Entrepreneur Magazine. The draw was the idea of a kid learning music at a young age, getting exposed to the realities of live music, and maybe learning an instrument they would never have otherwise picked up. The bonus would turn out to be maybe even more beneficial, just like Timmy Ramen was for us. If you think Hansel would be as good at public relations or rambling on his many podcasts about the company if he hadn't been the singer for Timmy Ramen, we'd remind you of just how off-key Hansel's karaoke was. That's the kind of confidence you get from being on stage in front of an audience who loves every minute of your act – even if it's just for the night. And that bonus of gaining confidence can be a life-changer. So in 2012, Hansel bought and operated a School of Rock franchise and started rockin' out, yet again.

As for the start of theCoderSchool, it happened about a year and a half after Hansel opened School of Rock. As so many things do, theCoderSchool had some family inspiration. Hansel's oldest, Maile, was 10 at the time, trying to learn to code

Hansel and family at the School of Rock opening

online through Khan Academy. It was fine enough, considering there weren't a lot of options even in Silicon Valley for kids to learn coding. But the more Maile coded, the more Hansel realized she didn't *really* learn anything about coding. Learning to code online isn't really learning if you're, well... not learning. Kids have this innate ability to just click to get to the end of a lesson, skipping over the main part – actual understanding of the material.

A lightbulb went off, and Hansel had the idea to fill that gap. Why not teach coding the School of Rock way – with a teacher sitting next to a kid, teaching them using music they like (or in this case, a game they like), at a speed suitable for them, and get them *wanting* to learn? What if you could also build confidence in a kid and teach them a skill that, statistically, they're going to need in the future? What if Hansel could start a School of Coding?

The Custom Vibe Company

Thus, in 2014, theCoderSchool was born. theCoderSchool teaches kids – usually ages seven to seventeen – to code. In other words, how to program computers to do what they want. Our biggest differentiator between us and our competitors? We treat each kid individually. Inspired by School of Rock's methodology, we tailor our instruction to each student's needs and interests. This contrasts with a traditional school's fixed curriculums and standardized teaching methods.

Early on, Hansel got a lot of unsolicited advice about this teaching style. Successful (i.e., rich-ass) business people, venture capitalists, even Hansel's own brother Haniel told him we *have to have* a *pedagogy*. Haniel even said "go look up that word, it's a real word." In simple terms, sustainable businesses were all about "repeatable and scalable" (i.e., have a detailed core curriculum that every franchise could push out). That's how businesses grow.

At a business level, it made sense – create a reproducible quality product, scale, and repeat. It's like how McDonald's controls their recipe for fries, forcing each franchise to cook them in a specific way. Sure, that's one way to control the quality of the product, but in our case, it would limit our ability to teach better. That's because we aren't selling the same french fries to everyone – we're selling individualized experiences.

Hansel always pushed back on the advice because his goal was never to grow as fast as we could, it was always to have a better product, to teach kids better. To make sure kids actually learn instead of just getting to the end. And the only way to do that is to be custom, not repeatable. In hindsight, this was one of Hansel's best decisions – stick with his gut, even if the rich-ass mofos said otherwise. Turns out this custom, bespoke style has permeated through every level of our company and is what we stand for today. Custom, customize, and be customizable.

One of our coaches early on was a break-dancer on the side, and he used some blue tape on the floor to show some kids how to read Cartesian coordinates. He'd have the kids tell him to go to different coordinates, and he'd get there while doing a break-dancing handstand. This is the kind of thing you can't put in a binder because you just can't predict what someone will bring to the table. As much as we'd all like to see it, Wayne sure as heck isn't going to start break dancing.

Even at the franchisee level, there's a lot of wiggle room and customizing. We encourage franchisees to focus on what they prefer, which may differ from school to school. One might be camp and workshop heavy, doing new things like YouTube camps or drone workshops. Another might be more technical and tend to teach private Java lessons for advanced kids. That's the magic sauce. Franchisees have a lot of leeway in our system because it helps them feel that ownership and accountability for their business.

That's not to say we don't have similar experiences – that's the power of a franchise. Even though schools are "custom," they all still run into similar problems with similar solutions. Most schools teach with the same platforms and languages because over time we've settled on what works best. And our scheduling tools, our notes tools, our brainstormed curriculum ideas, and most importantly the simple concept of "get to know the kid" are a must at every franchise.

Making the Team

Back in 2014, Wayne was still working at yet another of several start-ups, staying in the reliable 9-to-5 tech world. By then, we weren't hanging out a lot together anymore. Family and separate work lives can do that to a friendship, even if we had been through the Asian parties, Timmy, and FTV and other businesses together. Not long after Hansel formed the idea, we happened to take a guys trip to Vegas together, and naturally we talked about School of Rock since Hansel was neck-deep in it then, and theCoderSchool idea was still being formed. Wayne was even thinking about maybe buying a School of Rock himself. But 2 buffets and a few drunk nights later, the seed was planted. Hansel emailed Wayne after the trip and said hey – what if you joined me at theCoderSchool?

The funny thing is, Wayne wasn't even the first person Hansel asked to join him. That's how far they'd drifted apart by then. The thing Hansel realized while running School of Rock is that it's lonely at the top. Now the "top" of SoR ain't that high, but still, when you're the only owner running a business and making all the decisions, it can get lonely. Especially when it's a brand-new company. After Hansel's tech-savvy friends, Don and Brian, declined to join theCoderSchool, the third recruitment attempt proved to be the charm. If it wasn't for those first two rejections, theCoderSchool would likely be a very different company today.

Vegas and Hansel's enthusiasm were a hypnotic combination, but Wayne wasn't quite ready to dive into a new company yet – what if it was another Cheeky Chink failure? Wayne ran it past a buddy in venture capital, basically an early retiree because of all his investment and tech success. All three of us soon connected and decided to have lunch on the idea. It was Wayne, Hansel, and an Asian dude named Alex Poon. We'll leave all the jokes to you – our t-shirt making days are over.

Lunch was at a fancy country club in Los Altos, California. Some of the fanciest techies live there, like Sergey Brin, co-founder of Google. Or Yuri Milner who bought a property in Los Altos Hills for $100M in 2011, then the most expensive house sold in the country (of course, shortly after that, it was valued at "only" $50M). The weather could only be described as the perfect sunny California weather everyone dreams of – not too hot and just a slight breeze in the air. Picture it: two best friends, having outdoor lunch with a successful tech investor, over a business idea.

When you're talking to a guy who defined Silicon Valley success and are surrounded by it in a Los Altos country club, it's hard not to be drawn in by the whole thing. It didn't hurt that Alex's kids were young coders, too, and he was pretty psyched about the idea.

We were drinking Arnold Palmers and eating juicy burgers when Wayne realized that even if this thing fails, this was just the first of many fantastic lunches together. This was going to be our daily life. We wouldn't just be seeing each other at our kids' birthday parties anymore. If nothing else, we would meet and work together again like in the days of FTV, just like best friends were meant to do. That would already be hard to turn away.

At the end of the lunch, we said our thanks to Alex for his advice and headed to the parking lot for our debriefing. In the parking lot full of shiny new Teslas, dollar signs reflecting off of everything, Wayne took the final step and locked it in. "I'm totally fuckin' IN!"

Authors' note: When they make the anime version of the movie, that bold statement comes with a fist pump so strong it tears off Wayne's sleeves as he jumps into the air, kung-fu style.

One of the other reasons Wayne got on board was it wasn't going to be a huge risk for him, so on hindsight, we're not sure why Wayne was so hesitant. Maybe it was previous failed companies, maybe it was his brother Sandy saying the idea wouldn't work, who knows. Wayne would keep his tech job and salary from Oracle, where he worked at the time because they were insanely flexible about his hours (in other words, most of the time, his boss "worked remotely" too). In fact, he kept the Oracle job three years into working full time at theCoderSchool before finally getting a severance package. If there's a lesson to be learned here, it's to never quit a full-time salary without another in its place, though Hansel totally missed that lesson.

Of course, since this was going to be a legit third marriage, we needed to get Wayne's wife's blessing. Hansel is one to hit every detail, and knowing how this would change Wayne's life one way or the other, it was a detail he needed to confirm. Hansel even asked Wayne if he had any credit card debt (no) and gave him the third degree about how he spends his time (with family).

At the 4th birthday party for his daughter, Ella, while the Bubble Lady stole the show with her expert soap dispensing and blowing, Hansel pulled Winnie aside for a private conversation without Wayne. Hansel basically asked for Wayne's hand in marriage. This was going to be a big commitment – more time at the office, meaning Winnie would have to do more work with the kids. This was a second job that would hopefully become Wayne's only one, but there were no guarantees. If we told you she said no, this would be a hell of a way to pull the rug out from under you. But clearly, the tCS family grew that day and doubled in size – to two.

Palo Alto

Because of School of Rock, Hansel's learning curve for starting up wasn't huge. It was a really similar business, except for the material taught, of course. He even got permission from the higher-ups at SoR to start tCS. The only untested part was a pretty big chunk of it – coding.

Weirdly enough, even though we were in the heart of Silicon Valley, there was no physical space where kids could go to learn to code at that time. Hansel saw this as an amazing no-fail opportunity, while Wayne saw it as proof it might not work. Despite, or perhaps because of, that strange balance of unbridled optimism with useful practicality, we were going to go for it.

Hansel and Family opening the first school

The first location was always going to be Palo Alto, where Hansel lived, whether Wayne joined or not. Palo Alto's another uber techie place, perhaps more than any other in Silicon Valley. It's where Mark Zuckerberg and Larry

Page live. Even Steve Jobs used to live there – his wife still throws the most amazing giant Halloween party for the public at their house, big enough that it made the *Washington Post*. Palo Alto is also famous for being where Hewlett and Packard (and many more since) built their company out of their garage. It's even where the HBO show *Silicon Valley* was set. Palo Alto is in the heart of the real Silicon Valley, and if you think about it, the techiest part of the techiest place on earth. What better place to start the first location of our coding school?

The Grand Opening was on a Saturday afternoon in August and lasted two hours. In a word, it was insane. It was elbow-to-elbow with barely room to move, and scary-full of parents trying to throw their credit cards at us before the spots sold out. If we had time to look at each other, we would have said holy cow, we fell ass-backwards into something crazy. Fortunately, we were prepared – mostly – even if Wayne was sort of freaked out. Imagine all your customers lining up to ask you questions on day one about this business that didn't exist the day before. No pressure.

That's why all of our answers felt like 1,000% vaporware. In the end, most answers turned out to be right, but when you've never run the business before and there was no such business yesterday, honestly, all your answers are probably BS in some way. Yes, kids will learn the best in our no-curriculum approach! Of course, they'll progress in a few months! Parents wanted to know how it all worked, how they'd see results, and why there wasn't a curriculum. So we'd just blurt out whatever was at the top of our heads, and end it with "kids really need to learn to code, right?!" And the parents would just agree and say, "awesome, where do I sign up?" We teach our franchisees to do this, too – if you don't know, it probably doesn't matter yet, so say something the parent will agree with. We know it can sound and feel like BS to you – but we've been there, and now we know – it's not BS, what we're teaching you to say is true. It isn't bullshit, it just feels like it until you've actually done it.

At some point, the place was so full that people just spewed out of the building into the parking lot, so one of us went outside to answer questions. It was only us two who could answer the questions, so picture each of us being surrounded by a mob of parents wanting to know what tCS is all about. We'd get tech dads who are engineers, asking us if we'd heard about the latest "Docker to Git platform integration" or whatever, basically trying to show us how smart they were. Or someone asking us who owns the intellectual property if one of the kids builds a million-dollar app (spoiler alert, they will not).

Some of the most common original questions aren't asked anymore, like "How do you know tCS will work?" or "Will the kids *really* learn this way?" We took our fair share of sweating bullets for those questions in the beginning so our franchisees wouldn't have to later. After teaching many tens of thousands of kids across the country, people get a pretty good idea that we have our act together, so they no longer ask.

Hansel was the school's manager once we got going, having laid out the framework for how the company would operate based on his School of Rock experience. Wayne started out as a Code

Coach so he could learn the ropes and get ready to open his own location in San Mateo. Wayne sucked up all the knowledge he could on how to run the business, from how to teach to how to book the revenue and more. To both of our surprises, the original model that Hansel created in 2014 is really the same core model we run today. As we like to say, a lot of nice ass-backward falling is happening here.

Things only went up from there. After the opening day, we had upwards of 70+ students right away. Not a lot of businesses are profitable on day one, but we were lucky enough to have that happen. That first deposit of about $11,000 felt amazing and is something we would have loved to have framed if it wasn't all digital.

So, with that start, Hansel said IZZZON and pushed Wayne to start moving on the San Mateo location almost immediately. "But I'm just in the middle of figuring out how to coach," said Wayne. Stressful? Yes. But we also knew we were onto something. We could feel it in the air. Good timing combined with more good timing, combined with some backward asses, and we knew it would be stupid to wait. Suddenly, we went from Hansel's school with Wayne's help to theCoderBros, almost overnight, and we couldn't have been happier about it.

Chapter 7

Lather, Rinse, Franchise

Wayne and Family opening the second school

There might not be a word in the English language for the level of anxiety Wayne was feeling as he realized he had five months to open up an entire school in San Mateo, after Palo Alto had just gotten off the ground. Wayne was effectively our first franchisee – our first experiment to see how easily theCoderSchool model could be taught to someone who had never run a small business before. Or maybe to put it into Chinese terms, how many ai-ya moments do we need before someone learns how to run a school. Ai-ya, for you white people, is basically the universal Chinese phrase for "Aaaaaaaaaaah, fuck." Or if you're super disappointed, ai-yoooooo, as comedian Jimmy O Yang would say.

We would first connect with Mike Meffert, a super experienced agent in commercial real estate. Picture a middle-aged guy with a mustache, coffee in one hand, binder in the other arm, great with details, and about the most easy-going guy you could meet. The thing with renting a commercial space is it's not like renting an apartment – that's why we all need a Mike.

For one thing, all commercial spaces are zoned according to the city's standards – we need to be sure a kid's business is allowed there. That's why if you look around your city, all the businesses are in one area, and homes are in another (usually). Cities plan it that way, to account for things like traffic and parking (something Civil Engineers do, in case you ever wondered).

For another, a commercial lease is usually way more complex than residential ones. They often involve longer terms, typically 5-10 years, and can include additional responsibilities for tenants such as paying property taxes and insurance. The lease may also specify who covers renovation costs. Importantly, these leases never include provisions for business failure, so you better keep that business running. We always need a Mike who can help us understand and negotiate all this complex stuff.

As Mike and Wayne drove around to tour different spaces, Wayne would always have this blended feeling of elated excitement and primal fear. Getting closer to opening a new business will do that to you. Where he'd land on that wheel of emotion depended on the space they toured. There was a space they found on the 3rd floor of an office building. Hansel dang-near hung up the phone on hearing that one – definitely not the right fit; we need visibility and openness, typically a first-floor space with lots of windows. Then there was one downtown where a homeless guy started peeing at the end of the block – we took that one off the list pretty quickly. Some were too expensive, others were in a bad location – in short, it's a Goldilocks adventure, and Wayne was right in the middle of the story without an ending in sight.

Finally, Mike came across a vacant business that wasn't even listed. He took a shot – found the landlord, and just called. It turned out that the landlord didn't even realize the tenant had moved out already – commercial leasing can be chaotic. The beauty of that chaos is that sometimes, you find something that others don't. The space they found was the right location, the right visibility, and the right rent, too. We often tell our franchisees you never know what diamond lies in the rough. It may seem like you're out of options – but look hard enough, and you might find something unexpected.

Wayne (and Hansel, too) was stoked to find the perfect space. But as Wayne dove into a lease negotiation, he found the fear creeping up again. In most of America, a commercial lease comes with something called a "Personal Guarantee." It means if the business fails, you have to keep paying rent out of your own pocket – even if your business is dead. It's a little more lenient in New York, through a "Good Guy Clause," you can be released from a rental agreement. But for the rest of the country, it's an "incentive" for the landlord to "allow you to be their tenant" (even if we tenants are paying them the money!). We think of it as a Squid-Games-like test of your sheer resolve. In a 5-year lease for $5,000 a month, you're on the hook for *at least*

$300,000 of rent, usually much more - personally. That's what Wayne pictured as Webster's definition of signing your life away. But when you have your best friend behind you supporting you (or perhaps pressuring you), it somehow makes the decision a little easier. Well, maybe only slightly easier – but whatever the case, Wayne held his nose and signed the lease. Come hell or high water, this was happening.

Next up is where the poop can hit the proverbial fan, if you're not lucky – building permits. Almost every town has very specific requirements on how you can build out a space, whether it's your house or a business. Generally, they want to make sure what you're building is safe, especially when it comes to businesses that service the public. Move any walls or touch electrical, and you can bet you'll need to wrestle with the city and get a permit – otherwise, you're busted and fined. These permit guys (not to mention the inspectors they send out) basically have you by the balls and hold all the power. Permits can take a few weeks or many months (one of our locations was out of commission for over a year). It's the part you have no control over and can only curse at the building-permit gods when it doesn't go your way.

We weren't lucky, and our guy redlined everything, taking revenge on the world for some unnamed offense. He started off strong, saying we have all these "school" requirements like extra thick fire walls, new safety exits – the works. All because we had the word "school" in our name. It looked like we were going to be forced down a path that would cost many more thousands.

Luckily for us, Wayne's wife, Winnie, is an attorney. She found the permit wording in the official city code and argued that we weren't really a school (not one that takes care of kids all day anyway), but rather just an after-school "business." Something we learned – lawyers aren't ALL bad. Some of 'em are awesome.

We got lucky after that, and permits and inspections came mostly on schedule, even if the budget (about $50,000 to build out the space) was a little bit over. When we launched in February, our opening was again elbow-to-elbow. The space was a lot bigger than Palo Alto, though, so we avoided having people spill out into the street. That euphoric feeling of a job well done was the same – people everywhere, and us feeling like we again fell butt-backwards into this amazing thing. The difference is this time we had about 6 months more experience than before, so it didn't quite feel like as much BS as the first time. We again got a ton of new signups, this time thanks to Winnie's big social circle. It was a lot like bringing in our friends from the Asian parties to watch Timmy Ramen kick a little ass. An investment, an invite, showing everyone a good time, and blowing the place up.

The thing about marketing and getting the word out for our first two locations is that it wasn't the same. In Palo Alto, we had Hansel's parent list from School of Rock and also a coding club that was super generous in emailing its members. In San Mateo, it was a network of parents, and the yard signs Wayne put around. It's the same business model, and in this case, the same people running it – but what brings people in is always a bit different. There's no single marketing channel that works for every location or every person – you just have to try them all. In other words, you have to work to get the desired result, even if you've done it before. Marketing is a fickle beast; you can never rest on your laurels. You want customers? Then get to work.

At the end of the grand opening, Wayne felt something new – optimism. Even though Wayne had never run his own brick-and-mortar store before, he learned fast. "What do I do with this stack of paper sign-ups?" was the first issue at hand. The fact that there were so many that it required a process was a big win in itself. Imagine about 60 parents, each wanting a different time, and us trying to match kids up in coding pairs and then confirming the time with parents. That's when Hansel coined the term "Schedule Tetris". Except instead of the screen flashing when you lined up four in a row, it was our bank account. We were batting 1000 here – two for two – and ready to cash in on a third.

Our Third Kid

We started counting our schools in pics. Cheesy? Yep.

With #1 and #2 under our belts, we were confident – nay, cocky. With this seeming to be a slam-dunk business, we thought we had some wiggle room. To test our model's scalability, we decided to open a location in a city further away at a location we wouldn't manage personally. That begged the question: do we just fork over our own money – $70k or so – and just open this third location ourselves? Or do we test the investment waters, and see if it's worth it getting someone else involved? We'd be taking their money and running with it, and under the gun if we didn't profit soon enough. Since we knew this was a test, we went to someone we knew pretty well.

We put together a pitch deck with all of the details of how we make theCoderSchool work and how that would translate to success in another location, and we brought it to Hansel's brother, Haniel. Seeing the potential, he invested $100k to get us started, making him a 50/50 investor. If you ever watch Shark Tank, you would know that imputes a value of $200,000 for the business, meaning because he got 50% of the company for $100k, it was worth $200k. For us, we didn't put in any capital – we contributed our business model and operational expertise, using the investment to launch and run the new location. In return, we'd give up half the profits. Or if you're a "glass half full" kind of person, we'd *get* half the profits.

Our third location would be in Cupertino, far from either of our homes, and famous for being the HQ of Apple and the location of its spaceship offices. Also famous, at least in these parts, for being *very* Asian – in fact, over 70% Asian. A slam-dunk market for a slam-dunk business, right? As it turns out, we now see the "Asians" (yeah, of course we are generalizing and being racist here...) as a double-edged sword. Sure, they tend to be academic, education-focused with the tiger moms that force them to code. But those same tiger moms also tend to hover and suck the fun out, and those Asian dads often are cheap like us and would rather just teach their kids to code themselves. And some are at the balls end of cheap, like the Asian dad that walked into our opening, nonchalantly grabbed an entire box of Krispy Kreme donuts, and just walked out. And so, as we learned more about our own Asian kind, we started to learn that, for this and other reasons, Cupertino was not the automatic success third location we had in mind.

For those of you who have more than two kids, you know this part already. That third kid, they get the short end of the stick. There's never as many videos of them, never as many pictures, not nearly as much attention paid or spoiling of the baby. The parental excitement factor has waned because they've seen it all before. And our Cupertino location was our third kid.

Even before our opening, it was starting to show. We didn't respond to leads as fast as we did for our first two. Or we used boilerplate responses instead of personal attention to each interested parent. Hansel punted a to-do list to Wayne, who then punted the list right back. Along with 3rd child syndrome, Cupertino was also suffering due to our Overly Cocky Syndrome. As a result, this opening was *not* elbow-to-elbow, not a bunch of parents breathing down our necks as we'd found in our first two locations. It was successful enough, but the number of signups was about 20, as opposed to the 60 or 70 signups we got at each of the first two. This was a quick lesson that there are no gimmes in business. You can't just open the doors and get automatic success, even if the model worked before. The less care you put into it, the less you're going to get out of it.

After a relatively slow start, we still hadn't quite learned our lesson. Cupertino was a slow-grow kind of school, a school that just didn't get the attention we should have given it. We were trying the remote model, where we hired a manager to run the school because we couldn't be there. It was a blunt Bruce Lee nunchuck of a lesson – the difference between a hired manager and an owner who has their own money on the line is stark. It's hard to have that passion and fear needed to run a business if you're just a manager getting a salary. Finding the right manager who has that passion is one of our biggest challenges. While our system today has a handful of amazing ones, a good manager is still as elusive and hard to find as ever.

Luckily, we didn't need to pump in more money, but it did take a long time to get Cupertino to profitability. At a certain point, our investor Haniel happened to be in between CEO jobs. So, probably bored out of his mind (he was building a life-size Lego Batman at the time), he started asking about his investment. Next thing you know, we're giving monthly updates to Haniel to lay out all the metrics and strategies we were using to get this thing profitable like we're in some investor boardroom. No offense to Haniel, but that was probably right about the time when Wayne decided not to get another investor, and Hansel decided not to work directly with a relative.

Shortly after that, we got an amazing manager John, who has a Computer Science degree from Stanford, and low and behold,

Cupertino started cruising. By the writing of this book, Haniel has made his entire investment back and is getting anywhere from 20%-40% return almost every single year on top. We dare you to find any investment near that good (no, lucking out on buying Nvidia stock does not count). Not a year goes by when we write that check that Wayne doesn't say to Hansel, "Man, we need to find an investment like that."

As mistakes go, one of Hansel's biggest happened with Cupertino, apart from the lackadaisical opening. He was so sure of Cupertino's impending success (again, we be cocky) that he signed a ten-year lease. Now a ten-year lease in and of itself isn't unheard of. But it's a gamble – you're locked in at a certain rent, and you're gambling that the rent you're paying will be lower than others in 10 years. Alas, the gamble was a fail-and-a-half, and Cupertino, 9 years later, is now the highest rent of all locations everywhere, over $8,000/month for a space that's less than 1,000 square feet. Scary-stupid high rent. Even with that, and dick landlords who didn't help at all when the pandemic started (we were paying $8,000 a month to *not* come in), we've managed to pull a profit ever since we got John in there. The lease is up soon though, then we're flipping the mighty bird to that space and moving the heck out. No more ten-year leases for us, the flexibility of a shorter lease is worth more than a roll of the dice on slightly lower rent. But damn, I mean ai-yooooooo, right?!

Beyond Cupertino

Back at the San Mateo opening, one of Wayne's friends got really excited about theCoderSchool. "You guys should franchise this, I'll be your first!" Christian said. Truth be told, at the time, Hansel pushed back on the idea. This was only our second school; we weren't ready with a proven playbook yet.

Ironically, our current largest competitor Code Ninjas thought the exact opposite – they started franchising even before they opened their first school. We had a chance to ask them how they could franchise without ever having tried their playbook first, and they basically said hey, it's coding for kids - tCS is already doing it so what could go wrong?! For them, not much, because today they have a lot more locations than we do, and their original founder cashed out and made out like a bandit.

But for us, we've always thought that slow and steady wins the race. Do what's right, and you'll get yours in the end. We've never judged ourselves on the number of locations, rather we focus on the quality of teaching and the ability of our schools to be profitable in the long term. So while Hansel did push back when the idea first came up during opening number two, a few months after opening number three, Christian's idea resurfaced.

It was a chilly afternoon at the Starbucks on University Ave in Palo Alto. Despite the cold, we sat outside, under a cloudy California sky. We met, just the two of us, with one item on the agenda – do we open more of our own or do we start franchising?

The choice is similar for most companies. Opening our own means we'll be managing a big team and we'll likely need funding to move fast, but in the end we'll likely be making a lot more money (if we're successful). On the other hand, franchising means setting up the franchise system, but it's other people's money, risk, and profit (mostly). Opening schools on our own could mean about 5x more profit for us, but we'd be a real company with offices, teams that report up, and all the risk and headache of having 20 or however many "babies." Franchising means owners who have their own money on the line, so each owner gets to have their own first child, with the passion to match.

For us, only one option fit our personality, let us run a lifestyle business while helping others succeed, and, most importantly, allowed us to scale the passion that a business like ours needs. By now, you know the answer – we downed that Americano and Mocha Latte, got a big caffeine buzz, and started down the franchising path.

Chapter 8

All That Heavenly Glory

———✦———

Maybe you understand franchising at a high level already, but we thought you might want to hear a bit more nitty-gritty detail. It's like Bruce Lee said in *Enter the Dragon*: "It's like a finger pointing away to the moon. Don't concentrate on the finger or you will miss all that heavenly glory." It's a little high-minded to call the details of franchising "heavenly glory," but Bruce hasn't steered us wrong yet.

Franchising, at a 10,000 foot level, is when a (usually) successful business sells their playbook and support to someone else to help them start their own location of your business. Franchising means selling (renting, actually) logos, branding, business plans, everything it takes to run the business, including the support needed – to franchisees. The franchisees get a head start in building their own business instead of needing to figure everything out from scratch.

The franchisor isn't the "boss" of the franchisee, they're more like a consultant, someone that helps the franchisee become successful. McDonalds is a franchise, as is Subway, Kumon, Fast Signs, and thousands of other companies. That means the locations you see are probably owned by a local business owner, with the corporate headquarters being the franchisor supporting them.

Franchises can run in different ways under the covers, but there are several things that make theCoderSchool similar to other franchises.

Royalties are the big player for any franchise. This is how we get paid, like how an actor or musician keeps getting paid. For example, every time that Simu Liu commercial about Google Pixel runs on TV, he gets a few bucks (eh, maybe more than a few) as royalty. For us, the proven playbook, brand, and support is what we're selling, so every month we get a percentage of the total revenue of each franchise as our royalty. In our case, it's 5%. Unlike with Simu, it's not exactly "passive" income because we have to continually support and improve the brand. 5% is a lower rate than most of our competitors because that helps our franchise owners be more successful (i.e., profitable). Hansel always says what keeps him up at night is the success of each franchisee – not whether we're making the most money. So we do what we can to give our franchisees an edge. Never mess with the golden goose.

The **Brand Fund** is also a common expense at many franchise systems. Many franchisees feel this is a "cost" that goes to us, and it is – but it isn't. A Brand Fund is a franchisor's way to pool marketing dollars from all franchisees to run larger ads that single locations couldn't (one day, Super Bowl, baby!). It floats all boats, so to speak, almost a required minimal marketing spend so the brand as a whole is elevated. Ours is only 1%, which is lower than the typical 2-3% of our competitors. You can argue whether that's good or bad though, a high brand fund used well could mean more brand recognition and more customers for everyone. While it's always written in franchise contracts that we could pay ourselves extra from this fund to administer it, we would never do that. If we wouldn't want it done to our cheap asses, we wouldn't do it to someone else.

Then, there's usually an **Initial Fee**. There's an upfront cost of about $30k to start a franchise with theCoderSchool. That may seem like a lot, but it covers all the things we need to do to get a new location set up, like initial training, site selection, and just plain getting people in the system. It also offsets other costs that grow as the system grows. Annual insurance, legal fees, and other administrative stuff can easily cost well into the six figures for a franchisor like us, and it's a cost that grows as the system grows. Other systems go another way, like Kumon. Kumon charges a very low initial fee and even subsidizes some costs like furniture and signage, allowing owners to open on the cheap. A great model, as owners can get started without much funding. But then they get you in the back end, where the effective royalty is quite a bit higher (20-30% of revenue, depending on how you calculate it). Business is business, but you can't knock that model, with over 26,000 locations as of this writing!

Finally, the big picture number is really your total **Startup Costs**. We won't go into *all* that heavenly glory here because there's a lot. But think security deposits, build outs, permits, insurance – there's a giant list of things you need to do to start your own business.

You'll find food franchises (the ones with all the equipment) tend to, of course, cost more upfront. $2,000,000 or more is not uncommon to build out a White Castle (yep, we thought about it – but they don't franchise, unfortunately). Something like us though, you'd be looking in the $70k-$150k range (our legal doc has the actual estimates), but it is a *range*.

While some folks think there's a range because different areas of the country have different costs, it's actually not that at all. It's how good you are at being Chinese (i.e., finding the good deals). One guy paid $150,000 to build out his space – he was pretty fly for a white guy. But then we had people who built out their space for $10,000 – they were pretty pleased with their Chinese. The cost of living in the $10k area was, ironically, way *higher* than the one that cost 15x more. It's proof that being cheap can pay off in the business world.

We love saving our franchisees money, so we've figured out a nice cheap-but-premium model, if there's such a thing. It's all about that paint scheme and décor, which we've perfected over the years. Hansel even required all franchisees to hire a designer in the beginning – but now that we've done it so much, Hansel designs the spaces himself for free, saving every franchisee that extra cost.

There are other costs too, of course. Some franchises force you to buy inventory or equipment through them so they can get a cut of that - that can sometimes add up. Or other more minor things like transfer fees, minimal tech fees, and other random stuff found in the contract. But you get the picture – it costs money to start and run a franchise. Sometimes the heavenly glory is just boring-ass stuff, and you just want to focus on the finger. Sorry, Bruce.

Should You Buy a Franchise?

Fair question, imaginary person. It depends on what you're looking for. Do you want the support of a proven system, someone to guide you? Or the freedom to go nuts and do what you want? Franchising is great because you're starting way above the ground floor and have plenty of support to keep you going. We'd be the first to say that even though we have a proprietary playbook, our business isn't rocket science by any means. We don't have some secret 11 herb-and-spice curriculum. But Hansel has built a pretty efficient ecosystem, and Wayne is pretty effective at helping our franchisees achieve success. Not all franchises have, or need, a secret recipe to sell – we've just done it enough to be pretty good at helping others be good at it.

In a franchise system, there's less probability of failure, too, with someone holding your hand and guiding you through all of it. The other side of that coin is that you are limited in what you can do in your business – franchise systems have guidelines to ensure consistency. That's not to say you can't make a lot of money – some of the richest people at the International Franchisor Convention were pulling up in their private jets because they owned a bunch of 7-Elevens. It just means you can't just up and decide to start selling instant ramen for profit from your coding school franchise.

A franchise is also a big-ticket item, so it's a big commitment in both time and money. Only about one in 200 interested parties ends up purchasing a franchise, largely due to the significant commitment required. Sometimes it's beyond just knowing it's a successful playbook. Sometimes once you really think, "do I really have the time and money to do this", that answer is no. You are, after all, "buying a job", with a commitment of 10 years (our franchise is a 10-year contract).

The difference between *this* job and a corporate job is you control all the levers. When you bust your ass and work really hard for a big company, you may – or may not – get recognized or promoted. Not so in a franchise, it's your business – you bust the ass, you make the money. Of course, on the flip side, if you're quiet-quitting at work, you probably still get that paycheck. Try quiet-quitting your own business, and you might find the profits are turning to losses. Being invested makes a difference.

That's because being invested means you're more likely to be successful. To be invested in your own business has big rewards, both financially and emotionally. Many of our own franchisees will tell you that. Seeing a 9-year-old fix a bug and yipping in delight is its own kind of reward. As are all the students who tell us how much we've impacted their growth, some of whom even come back to work for us. And, so is creating something (even if it is with someone else's help) by yourself, and watching it become successful. That's an amazing feeling. So, if you're looking to turn some passion into financial and emotional rewards while having someone in your corner helping you every step of the way – franchising may just be for you.

The Way of theCoderSchool

As Bruce Lee kicks butt in his own way in *The Way of the Dragon*, so do we at theCoderSchool. Most franchises at our size – about 70 locations as of this writing – might have a team of ten or more people on payroll. For us, a decade in, it's still just the two us running the whole show, with another half of one employee on staff. Sure, we have a few vendors and contractors – but by and large, the franchise side is our company, and the two of us own it 100%, and operate it (almost) 100%. That's why, you know, theCoderBros.

So why don't we have a big team like everyone else? First, it's not in Hansel's personality to be the CEO of a large company – and your core personality is important to how you run a business, which we'll talk about in a future chapter. Second is the Chinese Cheapo factor. Do we *really* need to spend money and hire a bunch of employees? Wayne is great at researching HR issues and has an HR lawyer to help back him up. He's also figured out encryption certificates, GoDaddy's servers, and even dove into Amazon's cloud servers for a bit. Hansel, in addition to coding all our custom software, has picked up web design, interior design, accounting, franchising legalese, google analytics, and anything else the company needs to run. The philosophy here is if you can pay someone to do it – why can't you just do it yourself?

Most people would say hire out everything and delegate. At theCoderSchool, we hire IN everything and never delegate. Not only do you save a lot of money, it also forces you to learn every aspect of the company. That means you can make smart decisions without relying on someone else's expensive time, and it means you know a lot more about how and why your company ticks.

We also have never rented a corporate office – we've always worked remote. We meet up in person weekly to talk shop and, if we're being honest, to just hang out as best friends and talk about our kids and upcoming vacations. But instead of paying for office rent, we meet at the nearby burger or pizza place (remember, there aren't any White Castles in California) and expense that work lunch instead. If we need to meet a franchisee in person, we just meet at one of our locations. Why spend the money renting a fancy office? There's no need to do stuff just to look good (well, not in this case, anyway).

This uber-cheap style doesn't work for everything, though. Hansel might know enough to be dangerous, but he ain't no lawyer and he ain't no accountant, so we're not going to get into legal trouble by pretending to be one. We did hire a lawyer to draft the necessary 150 pages of legalese to make our contracts legit. There's some serious language in a Franchise Agreement, and while we understand what it means, it would be plain dumb of us to write it ourselves. We're cheap, not stupid. Same applies to our accounting. Sure, Hansel does all the books and knows the expenses as any good CFO would – but we sure aren't going to rely on him to file taxes to the IRS. So even though there will always be some things you need to pay for, never toss anything over the fence without knowing what it is they'll be doing for you.

The thing is, the *Way of theCoderSchool* is not about making *more* money either – it's about our franchisees making more (which, granted, in the long run should make us more as well). That's why we don't spend money on marketing to open more locations, and instead focus on operational tools. Since we're not shooting for Unicorn status, that opens the door for us to take our time and do things ourselves. That, in turn, saves us money and allows us to run that Lifestyle Business that we've always wanted.

Franchising Bootup

Back in our storyline, it's 2016. We had just launched Cupertino and had hired managers to run our other two schools, too. By then, we had both gotten the operational train rolling, and our three schools were chugging along, teaching hundreds of kids. Wayne's job became jumping on those trains and keeping them rolling by managing the three schools. Hansel, on the other hand, was still sitting at the station – the new Franchising Station. His job was to focus on starting a new kind of train, a franchising train. By this point, this was standard work separation between us – Hansel gets it going, and Wayne keeps it going. So Hansel got to work.

Everything we read and everyone we spoke to when we first thought about franchising said we'd need about a million dollars in funding to create a franchise system. Hansel's first and only thought was "No way. Screw that." It didn't add up, and he could not, for the life of him, figure out where that money would go. On hindsight, that million dollars is likely often spent on hiring consultants, writers, and developers. In other words, spent on people. It helped that these were all things Hansel did in his previous life as a consultant and was comfortable doing himself. It also helped that he had some guiding principles from having been a School of Rock franchisee. The stage was set, and Hansel started that engine. I think I can, I think I can, he said to himself.

The logo and tagline Hansel trademarked

"I think I can" soon turned into "I definitely can," as Hansel dug in. Whether it was writing manuals, creating and trademarking logos, or just plain coding away at our website, Hansel used our tried-and-true method of do-it-yourself and dove in and did it. Instead of spending a million dollars to start up our franchising arm, in the end it only cost about $30k, the amount we paid a lawyer to draft our first Franchise Agreement, and our only non-trivial cost. While Hansel could maybe have given that a shot, too, it likely would have had too many Chinese jokes and too much nonsensical language to be legally binding, so we thought spending that money early probably would save us a lot in the end.

After about six months of heads-down building, everything was ready, the franchise train was chuggin', and we were ready for passengers. Sure, some of it was luck, like having a new idea at the right time or Hansel's having franchising experience from

School of Rock. But part of it was skill – being able to create new processes and to design and code. And part of it was personality – not every founder is Chinese-cheap like Hansel. The rest was riding that wave while not getting cocky (except for that first year with Cupertino) and embracing new opportunities when they arose. Turns out a number of opportunities arose pretty quickly, as soon as we were ready for them.

Chapter 9

What Goes Up

Growth is a pretty good metric for success, or at least the beginnings of it. At the end of the day, sustaining that growth is the real metric, but you do have to start out somewhere. Franchising is like any other business – it's hard to get that first client because there's no proof your business works yet. Finding franchisees willing to commit to your system, especially when you're not an established brand, is no easy thing. We got lucky though; we were in a space that had a lot of potential but not a lot of competitors (none, in the first year). That's a winning combination every time.

Our first few franchisees came by word of mouth – just people we knew or randomly found us. Come to think of it, the rest of our school openings mostly came the same way. From what we've heard, this was sheer luck in running the right business at the right time. Most franchise systems have to spend gobs of money to find their franchisees – we're super lucky that we didn't (and still don't) have to.

This chapter tells the story of our growth through our openings. While there's a story behind every opening, we won't get into every single one because death by boredom is definitely a thing. Instead, we've picked a few to highlight. Fittingly, we'll start with the first.

The First One

The first test of our franchising system was going to be the Seattle area. Christian, the guy who first gave us the idea to franchise way back after the San Mateo opening, was based in San Mateo and a doctor. But he had friends in the Seattle area: one was a successful lawyer, Billy, and the other was a tech guy, Te (pronounced "Tay"), who worked at Amazon.

Franchising was new to us, and we, of course, wanted to meet everyone in person first. So, we decided we'd fly up to the Seattle area to get a lay of the land. Our first time taking a plane trip to meet someone about franchising was so cool – just the idea of flying somewhere for our very own business was mind-blowing to both of us. When we arrived, we got the full tour. Billy had a Tesla, which back in 2015 was still one of the early ones out of the factory, and was equivalent to a big sign saying I AM THE MAN. We jumped in for a speedy ride in the new electric car and took a tour of Bellevue, an affluent suburb of Seattle. He showed us the super nice neighborhoods, elite schools, and country clubs, all places where potential customers would be hanging out.

By the afternoon, we had all drank the Kool-Aid. "We're gonna do this everywhere and take over the Pacific Northwest!" they all said.

Multiple Seattle locations, Tacoma, even down to Portland, Oregon. The Kool-Aid effect is real, people. So Christian, Te, and the two of us headed back to Billy's office and busted out the paperwork. Back then, DocuSign wasn't common yet, so Hansel wasn't even sure how to get the thing signed. So we went old-school with a 150-page printed document held together with a big black binder. With the paper still warm from the massive print, we signed on the dotted line on a big 10-person oak table in the middle of Billy's meeting room.

"This calls for a celebration!" Billy said. He then reached into his secret stash and pulled out his special whiskey. Billy had an extravagant collection of scotches and whiskeys and prided himself a connoisseur, basically a whiskey sommelier. Even if we didn't have the palettes to tell the difference, we both knew we were in the big leagues and drinking the good stuff.

"Everybody's taking a shot!"

It was 1 PM. But hell, by then we both thought they were about to blow up the Northwest on our behalf, so it was time to party. Why not? We took our shots, and that shit burned alllllll the way down to the belly. But it burned so good. We had the expensive stuff and were sitting in a fancy law firm conference room, and theCoderSchool just signed its first franchise agreement. No matter what happened next, we had done it. Hansel had created this thing out of thin-air nothingness. Someone said they wanted it, and they signed on the dotted line to pay us $30k. It's not a feeling either of us would ever forget.

We flew home in a daze after the signing. As soon as we landed, though, it was time to get to work – we needed to train them on how to run a school. Our first training didn't even have slides or summaries. We literally trained them using the 200 pages or so of boring manuals that Hansel wrote to get the franchise system started. Although training was back on our turf in Silicon Valley, we didn't have a place to do it since our own schools were in session. So we got a meeting room at the Palo Alto library – free, of course.

That pre-opening training was crazy because teaching kids is one thing, but teaching adults who you won't be watching on the job is something entirely different. We had no idea what we were doing, and they ended up forgetting 80% of what we trained them on. Nowadays, though, we're pretty good at it. But it's still the same deal. People forget 80% of what they're taught because there's just so much information. The only difference is that we know it's coming. And that's ok. The *real* training comes on the job, when they're actually operating their school, and Wayne and his team are supporting them in real-time. As Ben Franklin once said, "Tell me and I forget. Teach me and I remember. Involve me and I learn." There's always a lot of forgetting when you're just told to do something. But when Wayne shows you what to do when you actually need to do it for the business, you'll learn it.

After a month or two of weekly calls and helping the Seattle guys get the space built and ready, we finally flew back to Seattle to help with the grand opening. And we were *psyched*. This was our first franchise, and it was actually launching! We were blown away when we got to the location and saw the logo, the familiar set up, the green and yellow with the pictures of kids coding. It was a dreamlike moment for us to see someone else build the same thing we had built from scratch, almost a thousand miles away. Our franchisee Te said to Hansel as he pointed around the room, "Can you believe all of this shit poured out of your brain?"

We couldn't, really. It was cool as hell.

NorCal

One of our earlier schools in Northern California, our 6th franchise, had a tiny space – something like 700 square feet. The opening was really packed, and they had invited a national robotics winner to attend with her 5-foot-wide spinning death-metal robot, or at least it looked like that to us. Seven hundred square feet, killer spinning robot, kids everywhere, what could go wrong? Thank goodness, nothing – the killer robot only brought us luck for a killer opening. Ironically, even with such a small space (though they've recently expanded), this location has always been one of our top schools, with over 250 kids all year. Kids are small, right?! Jam 'em in, we say, and save on rent.

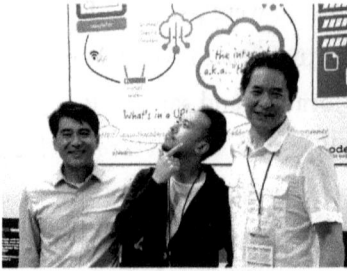

NorCal owners Lee, Allen, and Jim – all Asians!

The success of this school is no doubt in large part due to the manager, who knows all 250 kids and parents by name. He's so smooth, one of the parents who might have had a little too much wine was hitting on him at the opening – but don't worry, it was all PG-13. The owners are some amazing people, too, who were already successful in their own right. One was involved with local politics, one of those people who networked and knew everyone in town, even some presidential candidates. He also knows every ramen joint on the West Coast and could probably tell you who has the best tonkatsu soup in any 5-mile radius in California. Another owner was, among other things, part owner of a 5-star steak restaurant that counts celebrities like Steph Curry as their customers.

As much as we can't tell the difference between a White Castle slider and a dry-aged steak, they "forced us" to eat at that 5-star restaurant to celebrate their opening. When someone treats you to Wagyu beef and $25 drinks – you don't turn it down. Wayne gave them a 11 x 17 tCS poster in a $10 Amazon frame as a gift to congratulate them on their opening. When you compare our $10 gift to their $500 meal for us, it kind of makes you wonder how we get by in society, doesn't it?

SoCal

For our Southern California story, we fast-forward to our 16th franchise. This story might not start like something that belongs in a chapter called "What Goes Up" – but you'll see by the end that it does. We begin with their location. While Hansel does a lot of online demographic research, in the end, we leave it up to the owners, who know their local area best. And this was one of those locations – a bit hidden away, where Hansel probably said, "Weeeeeelllllll, if you *really* think it'll work there, it's your call." Marketing can be tough if you have to spend money or time on it. So if the location is in an easily visible spot with kids nearby with an easily visible sign with bright lights at night, it can help – a lot. If it's in an open, central spot, kids and parents are more likely to see the sign and, hopefully, be more tempted to try it out. This, shall we say, was not one of those spots.

The owners were some super-cool people, though. A mom-and-dad team, one with a meticulous, detailed mind, and the other a great communicator and community-relationship person (if you're super sexist, you can guess which is which). They did a lot of the footwork that some of the less-enthused owners typically don't want to do themselves, including reaching out to

SoCal owner Marcel giving us the thumbs

the community, putting up yard signs – all the stuff we still tell people to do when they open their own franchise. But, for whatever reason, not many people came out to their grand opening. By this 16th location, we knew good openings, and we knew not-good openings, and this was not a good opening.

To get a good deal on rent, the franchisees picked a location that was tucked away in a corner of this strip mall with barely any signage to point you in the right direction. In fact, when we got to the opening, we had to basically stand outside the space to wave people in – and there weren't that many people outside to wave in. Wayne had invited a buddy who lived nearby to come by and check it out, but he didn't make it. Afterwards, Wayne was relieved because, to be frank, the opening sucked. It was and always is a scary moment when the grand-opening hour strikes, and no one shows up. Then every minute that goes by feels like an hour. Tick-Tock, tick-tock, please show up. Sometimes we've even changed out of our tCS staff shirts so we can pretend to be a curious client and not have so much staff around. Eventually, some folks did show up, but it was definitely a bit underwhelming.

This is a "what goes up" story, though, and fortunately they did nothing but grow from that point on. We always say that the opening day can make you, but it won't break you. These SoCal franchisees just have a different energy – slow and steady wins the race, just like us. Today, this location is one of our strongest schools because the owners have the personality for it and have built an amazing product that the parents love and keep coming back for. The grand opening is a party, and sometimes the party is awesome and sometimes it's not – but that's separate from the business. You have to be the kind of person who can shake hands and keep smiling even if no one signs up, and you have to be the kind of person willing to work your butt off to offer an amazing product. These franchisees are those kinds of people, and they are and deserve to be one of our stronger owners in the system.

Despite our own concerns about the location, they proved to us that you can make a hidden school profitable. The bonus is once people know where it is, who cares where it is if the product is good? The parents will come. And if that rent is low, then you gambled on yourself and won. Where there's a will, there's always a way. Well, maybe usually a way. Willpower ain't magic.

East vs West

Our Long Island owners are worth talking about. At this point they could probably write their own book. We could tell from the first phone call that the group – a husband, wife, and sister team – were all about the passion. Hansel remembers saying to them that their passion and excitement literally spilled out through the phone during our conversations. They are one of the best groups at getting out in the community and just giving that good old-fashioned face-to-face customer service – gift baskets, personal phone calls, remembering names, the works. Heck, they actually look you in the eye and *listen* to you when you talk! You can't beat plain old relationship building like the old days. By now, one of the owners is practically a local celebrity because they do so much in the community. Whether it's a coding school, bakery, print shop, or any other small business, being good at communicating and working with the community is one of the biggest predictors of success.

We had flown out to support their opening and knew deep down it would be a big one, and they did not disappoint. It was the first time any franchise had an opening as big or bigger than our first, and it got us super jazzed. By the first day of teaching, they had 110 students signed up – way better than we ever did,

Madhouse opening with a line out the door

and a record that isn't likely to be broken. Considering that an opening event is usually only 2 hours long, that's almost one physical, in-person signup for every single minute.

The grand opening was organized like a well-oiled machine. They had thought of everything. They had greeters, coaches for the kids, video production, sign-up aids, food monitors – anything you could think of was there. There was a process for getting people in line, getting a quick coding experience, answering questions, signing them up, and then getting them right outta there. It was an assembly line for parents and kids, like a Disneyland ride on steroids, but the end of the ride was a signup. As we looked around the opening, we kept seeing their signup stations with constant long lines. They even had to bring out more signup stations to accommodate the line.

It was such a success that parents on opening day were already asking Hansel if they could open their own tCS location nearby, like *right now*. People know a good thing when they see it. As one of our favorite franchisees once said, "With great success comes everybody else thinking they can do it too." Hansel had already decided before flying out to the opening that the answer would be no – these owners were so good, we would hold all of Long Island for them to open more, without any deposits. Their awesomeness was good enough for us.

Checking out Short Hills with Zubair and Noreen from the Long Island Team

They've since had six more grand openings, for a total of seven locations – they're just that good at it. Every single opening has been huge, with sign-ups in the 50s, 60s, and 70s. Every opening has been that same well-oiled machine, with a process to get from A to B, coding to signup, in and out the door. They are handshake people, they are amazing communicators, and they love impacting kids and their communities. Interestingly enough, they don't like to delegate, but instead like to closely manage every single one of their schools. All a part of their success strategy. They started out in 2017, which means they've opened an average of one location per year since then. Each of their locations is in our list of top-ranked schools. They work their butts off like crazy, so they deserve all their success.

You'd think they're a unique bunch – and they are – but we have a West Coast equivalent. We like to call them rivals, just to, you know, stir the pot a little. The West Coast team is made up of one super-smart owner and some really amazing managers, including one who was eventually promoted to ownership. This team also has 7 locations as of this writing and is neck-and-neck with the Long Island folks. Their strength is different, though. Instead of being hands-on, the ownership team delegates to some top-notch managers who operate in their own lanes and bring most of their schools to our top-ranked list, just like their "rivals." It just goes to show you that a playbook can be executed in different ways to get to the top of the success chain. There's room for a Peyton Manning *and* a Tom Brady at the top.

Berkeley Snaps! Its Fingers

In our world, one of the best tools ever invented is called Scratch, by the mighty minds at MIT in Boston. It's a free-to-use programming language that aims to teach kids how to code by using draggable blocks that snap together. Developed circa 2003, this language is really the only reason a coding school like us can even exist. It makes coding so graphical and easy to learn that elementary-aged kids can create a legitimate game in a matter of hours, allowing them to get engaged quickly and have fun while learning to code at the same time. That said, Scratch isn't something you'd code a blockchain system with or use for a real business – but for kids coding, it's about as impactful as the invention of the iPhone.

Like the iPhone, Scratch kicked off plenty of copycats that tried to do the same thing but better. One of those copycats is a programming language called Snap!. At the end of the word *Snap* sits a "bang," as coders call it (rumor has it, because long ago the punch-card machine for old computers made a loud BANG when punching the "!"), as if beckoning you to do something amazing. Snap! was invented by a top computer science school on the West Coast – UC Berkeley – making for a nice rivalry with the Scratch folks from MIT on the East Coast.

The original Berkeley owners do a photo shoot for a spread in Entrepreneur Magazine

Back when our Berkeley school was opening, Hansel was doing a lot of tinkering with Snap! and lobbed in some upgrade suggestions through the website. To his surprise, someone actually replied. That someone was one of the two inventors of Snap!, Dr. Brian Harvey. Sensing an opportunity, Hansel used that initial connection to invite Dr. Harvey to theCoderSchool Berkeley opening, which happened to be just a week or two later. What better way to celebrate a coding school's opening than to have a real-life computer science celebrity attend?

Along with Dr. Harvey, it seemed like a million other people came to the Berkeley opening. The owners are great at going above and beyond – there was full-on dim sum and other delicious, real food for anyone lucky enough to come out. These franchisees are probably the best at staff and customer relationships, and they deservedly are consistently one of our top three schools in the country.

Like how we try to treat our franchisees right, they treat their staff and customers beyond right, if there's such a thing. Constant home-cooked meals for their staff, a huge budget for free snacks for everyone (inspired by big "startups" like Google and Facebook), and downright amazing customer relationships. One time we visited and saw the owners bear hugging someone like it was their best friend they hadn't seen for 20 years. Only it wasn't an old friend, it was a parent they had met as part of their business. That level of relationship with clients is the gold standard, something that damn near guarantees a successful business.

Bringing it Home

We're often asked, "Why haven't you opened a location in [insert city name]?" The quick answer to that is always, "No one from Minneapolis has reached out yet." We don't do marketing really, like targeting Google or Facebook ads to an area of the country where a tCS could thrive. We'd love to have someone from Minneapolis (or Philly, or Portland, or…) open a school. But instead of spending money to try to find them, we just wait for folks to find us. That way, they've already identified themselves as someone interested in the business, and they've probably already looked at our website and thought we're at least worth a chat. It may be a little slower, sure, but when you're not focused on growing fast, it's the most cost-effective way to do it.

That's not to say we haven't tried – it's not like we *hate* money. For a brief period, we had a part-time salesperson who would sell potential franchisees on the idea of tCS and sign them up. We hired her in 2018, and for what it's worth, 2019 was our best year for signing up new franchises. It wasn't cheap, but it wasn't crazy expensive either – up to $7k in commissions per location sold, plus a salary of about $40,000 per year. If she sold 10 new franchises, that's $70k in commission (plus $40k salary) to her – but it's also $300,000 in initial franchise fees to us. A pretty good deal for both sides, all in all.

But it never felt "right" with our brand. We wanted a mom-and-pop vibe, not a salesperson vibe. We've now gone back to Hansel taking on this role, including always being the first person to respond to any prospective franchisee who contacts us. Some people are definitely a bit surprised when the founder and CEO of a 70-location business is the first to contact them. But there's also some power to that because it immediately shows we really are a different kind of company.

More recently, we considered other methods. Not because we felt the need to sell faster, but just to make sure we weren't missing an easy opportunity. For example, we considered bringing in an investor who could start cranking the sales engine for us in exchange for a stake in the company. Maybe it would be worth it.

But nope, not even close. We realized investors wanted way too much equity, so we fell back to our default – we wanted our own lifestyle business we controlled, and growing faster was not worth giving that up.

We also talked to a few companies called Franchise Sales Organizations. It's like hiring a salesperson, only it's an entire sales operation with all the marketing power to not just sell leads but to bring in leads, too. We'd just sit back and wait for them to sign people up. Some of these guys sell 20-30 locations for franchisors in one year! It sounded like an amazing opportunity until we learned how much it *really* cost. The *lowest* cost we found was about $100,000 a year as a base, plus $25,000+ for each location sold. So if they sell 20 in one year, that would cost us $600,000! No knock against this model because we can see how the big-growth guys might make it worth the money in the long run. If you grow big and fast enough, you offset the high cost, and POOF! you're instantly a huge franchise system. But that was most definitely too rich for our blood, and definitely not the vibe we wanted for the brand.

Our process now goes like this. Someone finds our website and sends in their information. Hansel calls them and has a conversation. If the momentum is sustained, we send documents and then we talk again. And that goes on until both sides have enough information to make a decision. That's what it boils down to for us – conversations, just being real with each other. Before tCS, Hansel never considered himself a salesperson. Back when he was "just" an engineer, he thought of sales as a different and complex world. But now he realizes sales, at least for him, isn't made up of techniques to keep the buyer on the line or strategies to convince them we have a great product – you know, all those tips and tricks you might see on TikTok or read in books. For Hansel, sales boils down to genuine conversations and transparency about our business and values. That's all – just a simple, honest conversation. Of course, it helps to have a legitimate product to sell!

That's why the most important boots on the ground are yours. The sales and marketing conversations have to come from an honest place within you. If you don't have the passion to do it, if you're just chasing the money, or worse, you just want to automate it, that's when signs of failure might start to appear.

Chapter 10

Must Come Down

━━━━━◆━━━━━━━◆━━━━━

They say failure is the best teacher, so we've been schooled a few times – enough to know why locations might fail. When the first one happened to us, it was a punch in the gut – one of our kids was moving out of our family. And as we've gone on to close a few more, it's still a punch in the gut each time – just less so because it's something we now know is just a part of the business. It's a volume game – once a franchise system gets to a certain size, a location or two (or more) is bound to close. Whether it's a personal health issue, divorce, or just a loss of interest or passion, sometimes running a small business just isn't in the cards anymore for that owner. We understand this and will generally work with the owner to do what's best for them. From what we hear, our system has fewer closures than others, so we can always hang our hat on that completely subjective statement that we'll never try to prove.

The First One

Just as there was a first to open, there's a first to close. Our first to close was in an affluent area of the country, though not on either coast. It was a place where kids' education was important and, if we're honest, a pretty darn good location for a school. But this one had a combination of a crazy high rent (by now, it would have been even higher than our Cupertino location of $8,000!) and the thing that hit everyone – COVID.

This particular location also had a disadvantage in that it's run by a few investors. At least, we think that's a disadvantage. These investors were very successful in other kids' education businesses, and Hansel knew them before tCS – so how could it lose? As we've found out since then, it's difficult to run a community-oriented business like ours without rolling up your sleeves and really being hands-on with the passion of the operation. That's why we no longer allow investor-style owners to be franchisees. Now, these owners had been very successful at running a previous similar franchise, so it's not that they didn't know what they were doing. Maybe it's that theCoderBros (seems like we can talk about ourselves in the third person here, right?) just don't believe in the investor model, and that feeling permeated our system.

Being investor-owners, they were the first and still only owner group to ever open two schools at about the same time, within months of each other. That might sound great for us, the franchisor, to get things going more quickly, and buying/opening multiple locations at one time is a very common deal structure in franchising, called an Area Developer Agreement. With this agreement, the franchisee commits to multiple openings in a certain timeframe, and in return, the franchisor holds the territories for them – a tried-and-true formula for fast growth. But, you guessed it, this is something else we don't allow anymore either because it adds significant risk. Not to us, but to the franchisee. In case you haven't heard it from us yet – slow and steady, people!

We had known the location wasn't exactly performing well even before COVID. In the beginning, the manager they hired sounded great – but we found some major deficiencies after she was let go, only a few years after opening. When COVID came around, the overall franchise system was able to pivot to an online model, but this location had a tough go of it. Hansel remembers getting that email – "can we talk?" It's like when you're in a shaky relationship with a girlfriend, "can we talk" is the last thing you want to hear.

But talk we did. And just like a sales call, a closing call is the same thing – an honest conversation about where that party is at. What can we do to best support where you want to go, that's the sentiment that Hansel always has when we can. The truth is, although there's two legal commitments, these conversations usually revolve more around how an owner would be able to get out of the lease, not how they can get out of the Franchise Agreement. That's because for us, it's hard to milk much more effort out of someone who's lost interest – so we don't try, we just get on their side. But for a landlord, there's usually a personal guarantee that legally guarantees rent payments through the life of the lease, even if it comes from the tenant's personal pockets. This can be hundreds of thousands of dollars. And these landlords were trying to hold on to every dollar they could. It's easy to say the landlord was a dick for doing so. But it was mid-COVID, and landlords had a hard time, too, including potentially defaulting on their properties if they couldn't pay their mortgage because tenant rents were behind.

The landlord turned out to be a very large and powerful corporation, one that simply would not budge. They threatened to sue our franchisee for the entire remaining rent on that 10-year lease since during the pandemic there would be no way for them to rent it back out. And they would have won, too – there's no wiggle room in that lease. While the exact settlement amount remains unknown to us, we understand it was substantial, though less than the full lease obligation.

It makes you think twice about commercial leases, and how there are two sides to every story, often two valid viewpoints when there's a conflict. Knock on wood, this has (so far) been the one and only location that needed to close in the middle of an ongoing lease.

San Jose Goes Number Two

Our second closure, affectionately known as our pooper, or our number 2, was the first one after COVID and was in a coveted location in Silicon Valley, just north of San Jose. Luckily, they were able to close at the end of their 5-year lease, so they didn't have any penalties. The owners were a great couple. Really fun to be around, good folks. They had one of those blow-up dinosaur costumes at their grand opening, where the t-rex has a head that bobs around and tiny hands. You see those everywhere now, but back then, they were the trailblazers.

Hanging with the Dino

But as the school went into operations mode, they unfortunately weren't able to pay enough attention to the business. Though for understandable reasons – they literally had a new baby, and when that happens, guess which baby takes precedence? That's right, the real-life baby. We'd email, and they'd take days to respond. It made us wonder if they also took days to respond to customers. We hoped that they just chose to ignore ours because it was from us, but based on the school's performance, it probably was not the case.

The truth is, even before the baby, they weren't as focused as we'd hoped. They were great in person, but just didn't have quite the passion or interest level to get the marketing and signups going. So the school had generally slogged along for most of its years, despite a great location. They had great energy when we met them, great energy at their opening, but sometimes you just don't know if something is a fit until you do it for real. Job interviews don't mean squat – it's job performance that counts.

When they finally decided to close, another owner group quickly bought their territory. The literal day after this location closed, the new owners pounced on a new franchise agreement to open another, just down the road, in the same territory. And wouldn't you know it, it's one of our more successful schools today. It goes to show you, the local demographics don't matter as much as the execution.

Full Circle

It's a bit of a bummer that our first franchise (Seattle) ends up in this chapter, but it does because it eventually closed, too. That means all those dreams about taking over the Northwest didn't exactly pan out as we all had hoped. After Seattle started operating, a few things became obvious, though we didn't make much of it right away. You can spot a potential flaw, but until you know how your franchise system is going to work, you don't know if it's a fatal flaw or just something that will work itself out. It turns out that enthusiasm and financial backing alone aren't enough to guarantee success in franchising. It reinforced our belief in the importance of hands-on involvement and genuine passion from franchisees.

The first issue was their team dynamic; it was a little different than ours. We both pretty much share the load when it comes to what needs to get done, or one of us takes up slack based on our specialty. With this group, although they each owned equal shares, two were unable to help, leaving the third to operate it by hiring a manager. This was known going in, so no fault to anyone, but it's a tough model to have one person operate but only share 1/3 of the profits. On top of that, he also had a full-time job, meaning it was doable, but not exactly easy, for him to manage the school.

We've since learned that this kind of setup is a big risk. It's something we've warned other franchisees about – the person running the school needs to put forth the biggest effort, so make sure they get the biggest (by far) profit share. When you don't, the one who's short-changed will eventually feel it psychologically, and not have the incentive to work as hard. Now, is this what happened here? We don't know – we just know the structure wasn't ideal.

If you recall, we ended the Seattle/Bellevue story in the last chapter with us landing in Seattle, super-stoked to be there for the grand opening. There's a reason we stopped there and didn't talk about the actual grand opening because that story belongs in this chapter. As the grand opening went on, that euphoric feeling started to fade. It wasn't exactly one that was knocked out of the park. Some people did show, but it was the worst grand opening event we would see for a while.

We started to realize that night (there was no secret whiskey stash this time) that if someone wants to open a bunch of locations and all they have is money, it's a recipe for disaster. They've already worked for the money they poured into this business, and now they just want to throw that money at something that sounds cool. Now look, we still love those guys, and we can't say much bad about them. Hansel still keeps in touch with one of the guys (Te), and another (Christian) deserves a bunch of credit as the guy who nudged us into franchising. Good dudes all around. But because of this experience, nowadays if a new prospect comes to us excited about how much money they have to spend on opening so many schools, we run. Fast.

It took six years for the Seattle location to eventually close. It's a bummer because like our Pooper (aka our number 2), the Seattle area is also a great location with lots of kids and affluent parents. We're still trying to convince our West Coast rockstar franchisee team to open one in Seattle – and we so far have a firm definitely-maybe. As for the original location, they just couldn't quite ever get the right manager. Some were better with parent relationships but lacking in administrative tasks, or some were good at admin stuff but couldn't do the marketing. It's a common challenge we all have – finding a manager with all the right skills. It's tough to find that passion from a manager who isn't vested in the business, who will work to do all the right things. Never underestimate the passion (otherwise known as fear of losing money) of an owner. It's why plenty of franchise systems out there (but not us) require owners to operate themselves instead of hiring it out to a manager.

Who Gets the Hug?

Sometimes a business relationship is less than ideal. Not bad per se, but just not what either side expected. Austin seemed like a perfect location, as Texas's super high-tech hub. From the start, Amy, the franchisee, had a lot of questions. Why did we use this software? Why is your process this way? She had a lot of great energy – but it wasn't the same kind of energy we had, it was on a different frequency. We disagreed a lot on how our franchise is run. You can argue that she wasn't listening when we explained the whole system to her prior to signing – but honestly, it's back to what we said before. It's not the interview;

it's what happens on the job – sometimes you (both sides, actually) just don't know until you know. And, we were having enough disagreements that even Wayne, who goes with *every* flow, was feeling the pressure, too.

The first time we flew out to visit, we brought her Voodoo Doughnuts – an awesome donut chain that started in Portland but was also in Austin – as a little peace offering. Our relationship was already a little awkward after a number of back-and-forths about how or why we do things a certain way. As we walked up to the door, we had one of those inane conversations between two guys. Who would hold the donuts when we walk in the door? Because whoever isn't holding them has their hands free and would have to give Amy a hug hello and be the first one to break the awkwardness. A glimpse into the sometimes-stupid conversations two best friends have when they run a business together. After ten minutes of bickering, joking, and pushing the donut box back and forth while standing outside the school, Hansel lost the coin toss and had to give Amy the hug hello. It was one of those hesitant should-we-or-shouldn't-we kind of hugs that definitely broke some awkward tension.

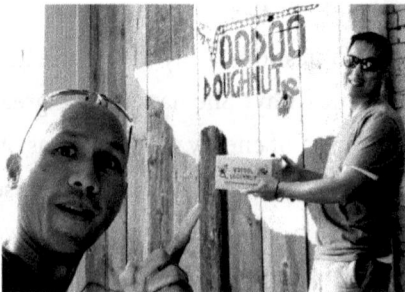

Wayne wins the coin toss

As bad as that may sound, it wasn't all that. We're embellishing for the book. The tension floated away as soon as we hugged. We like Amy, actually. We just didn't see eye-to-eye on how to operate a school, and that's okay – people can and should have different opinions. She wasn't about to close either, her location was doing fine. But instead of forcing her to get in line with the franchise standards, Hansel thought about what the best outcome for all parties would be. So he decided to do something a bit unconventional – he let her convert the school to her own coding business and essentially be released from the franchise agreement. This was by no means a financial decision – it's a bit dumb to let a franchisee in, train them on your methods, and then let them out of the system *and* all future royalties. All franchise agreements have this provision in place, you can't just take our playbook and become our competitor. But legal agreements be damned, sometimes that's the right play.

She de-branded by removing our logos and colors, but we actually let her keep some of the artwork. We still hear from Amy from time to time, and it sounds like she's still doing great with her school in Austin, running it her own way. Fittingly, it's called My Coding Place, so look her up if you live in Austin, and tell her we said hi.

The Great White North

Some locations are an abject lesson in how you should proceed as a business, and Toronto is one of those for us. These three Canadian friends were incredibly cool and excited to get moving on our first franchise outside of the US. They contacted us before we were allowed to franchise in Canada and convinced Hansel to do the paperwork to get us there. We were both super excited, too. Apart from it just sounding so cool – "*theCoderSchool is international!*" – it also seemed like a great steppingstone to open up to other countries. Plus, we'd get to see some cool places up in Canada that we'd never seen before, which means more cool trips with your bro. We were already practicing our Canadian lingo, "Let's grab a coffee at Timmy's, eh?!"

As our closest neighbor culturally, you'd think it'd be easy to set up shop and franchise in Canada. You'd be dead wrong. Canada's franchising rules are just similar enough to ours to reuse a lot, but different enough to drive you a bit batty. Franchise agreements needed a Canadian version and had to be updated for every single agreement signed (in the States, it's updated once a year). Then there's trademarks, which work differently in Canada. Canada has its own currency. They don't have background checks the same way we do. Not to mention tax implications of foreign income. But after spending upwards of $40,000 on lawyer and accountant fees (yep, costing even more than initial setup in the US), we were ready to give it a shot.

In February of 2020, our first Canadian franchise agreement was signed, and shortly after, the first lease was executed. Wait, February 2020? Yep, they signed on at the same time COVID signed on. At first, we thought they were absolutely screwed because they signed a legitimate lease, and all of U.S. and Canada were shut down. But as luck would have it, they got out of the lease. We ended up letting them out of the franchise agreement, too, because no one knew at that time when COVID might recede, or if it ever would.

After COVID, the franchisees asked about a new location a few times, but in time faded away and decided not to open one. In many ways, it was meant to be because by that point Hansel had given up on Canada – it just wasn't worth the effort and cost. The currency changes, the tax laws, the franchise rules – there were probably 20 other things we didn't think about once a franchise was operating. In short, it was a pain in the ass. After spending a total of something like $60,000 to get and continue to be set up for Canada, we killed that effort and no longer will franchise in Canada or any other country, for that matter. That's no easy decision because we already spent all this money and were approved and ready to go. But the continuous hassle to keep up with the laws just to get a few schools up north was not worth it. Sometimes you have to recognize when something is a sunk cost and know when to walk away. It was a $60,000 failure, but now we're also that much smarter.

Any business will have failures like these – it's part of the process of building something successful. Even with some failures – and hopefully by now you realize that a failure is a lesson more than anything else – we're proud of our franchises. We're proud of our playbook, too, because if it's followed, it makes it easy to keep those failures as lessons only, and not the end of what could be a really fun journey. Hell, a lot of our franchisees do better than our own three schools with that playbook, but we look at that as a good thing. Our job is to help the franchisees be successful and make money, so it's a win for us when they do better than us.

Chapter 11

Two Men and a Franchise

The two of us make up theCoderBros. And sure, it's about theCoderSchool as a business – but it's also about who we are as people and how we work together. Like how our business is run, how we work together isn't typical, either.

The Greek philosopher Epictetus once said, "Wealth is defined not by having great possessions, but in having few wants." He was talking about life, but we've adopted this for our business. We don't need to be a Unicorn business to be successful. We don't need an IPO, and we don't need breakneck growth, either. Success for us is a company that's secure, but more importantly, a company that can give you great life experiences. In other words, it's a lifestyle business. As far as we're concerned, Epictetus was Greek for "The Bruce".

Traditional thinking goes like this: if a company is valued at hundreds of millions of dollars on paper, with beautiful Class-A office spaces and high-powered employees closing deals, it's a wealthy company with "great possessions". That "wealthy" company, though, is likely consumed by an endless appetite for more. More profits, more growth, more investors, more stress. We see theCoderSchool differently. We don't have Class-A offices – instead, we open our laptops at a local fast food joint. High-powered employees? Other than us two owners, there's one employee – a part-time one at that. Most importantly, we're not greedy for more. We love the life we have, and the honest truth is that growth and more money isn't our main goal. Our main goal is to live our best life, without always wanting more. If that's wealth according to Epictetus, then we're wealthier than we could have ever imagined.

Now, do we have the occasional fantasy of an IPO making us crazy rich? Can we picture ourselves up there ringing the bell someday? Sure! (Well, Wayne can – that is his literal dream he constantly talks about – so maybe he still has a few wants...). Come on – who doesn't sometimes dream about sailing the world in a yacht while closing deals on a satellite phone? What people generally don't think about is the flip side of the dream, which is all the *other* stuff that comes with getting there. Making money by building a company to an IPO level takes sacrifice. Will you miss your daughter's tennis game? Maybe. Is there time to exercise, or will the stress impact your health and take years off your life? Probably the latter. Will making $1M per year *really* make you that much happier?

There's a famous study by Nobel prize-winning economist Daniel Kahneman that says it won't. In fact, according to the study, happiness peaks at a $75k annual income (granted, this was circa 2010 so don't forget inflation). After that, higher income doesn't actually make people happier. Happiness that comes from wealth is often temporary. It's like when you go on a shopping spree and at first, you're happy with all this new material *stuff*. But those feelings quickly fade. Compare that to the best date with your spouse, or the most fun road trip to Vegas, or the time your daughter took her first steps. The point is that experiences last a lot longer than money when it comes to happiness. Because of that, we try to focus on experiences over money when we can, and being able to is why we feel our business is "wealthy." Feeling wealthy in your business means a lot has to be aligned – lucky for us, it is.

The Same Dude

Our business is a legal relationship, but we're also best friends. We've got joint custody of all these franchises, and our job is to help them grow up happy and healthy. Call it what you will, but this thing is basically a marriage with lots of kids. And who doesn't want to marry their best friend? Sure, you won't always get along perfectly, but in any good marriage, you work things out. You have a lot in common, but you also have different perspectives, you complement each other, and you make each other better, just like our tCS marriage.

In many ways, we're the same dude. We both have a similar sense of humor, both went to WashU, both worked in high tech, both huge Bruce Lee fans, both Asians with a similar group of friends. And of course, both love White Castle.

When it comes to our business, we're both uber dedicated. If you email us, you might be surprised at how fast Hansel responds or how late at night Wayne replies. It's who we are, we

Got to Third Base after 10,000 dates

live and breathe tCS, even when we're on vacation with our families. It's not that work comes before our families (it doesn't), it's that tCS is so engrained in who we are, and it's (mostly) genuinely something we enjoy. The old adage of "do what you love, and you'll never work a day in your life" just happens to be super true for us.

We work with a best friend, travel the country together, and have a flexible schedule, so we feel like we're *already* retired. But this blurs the line between work and leisure. We're always "on" and always working, whether it's Sunday or family vacation time. It's like when we're working, we feel like we're on vacation, and when we're on vacation, we're still working. People talk about work-life balance as if they're two mutually exclusive things, like a pendulum that swings back and forth between work and play. Not us, we feel doing both at the same time is what sets you up for longer-term success. Thinking the same way means we have the same expectations of each other.

Opposite Dudes

But we're opposite in a lot of ways, too. A lot of romantic comedies are about two opposing forces who eventually come together to make something wonderful. Take *When Harry Met Sally*, an all-time classic. Spoiler alert here, but you knew from the beginning they were going to get together despite their opposite personalities. In the end, they got married, opposite personalities and all – not unlike us with theCoderSchool.

If you meet Wayne in person, you'll find he's really easy-going and quick to get along with. At his core, he's a go-with-the-flow kind of guy. Wayne epitomizes Bruce Lee's "Be Like Water" philosophy and is about as close to being like water as a human being can be without turning into a mermaid. When he comes into any situation – whether it's business, personal, or anything else, he's going with the flow. You tell him the sky is green, and he's likely to agree with you and give you props for noticing. If he comes upon a river, it doesn't matter if that thing has a rainbow at the end of it or if it's going over the falls; he'll plop in his floatie and just go where it flows. That's how Wayne's built.

Hansel's the opposite. If he comes upon a river, he'll test the temperature, read the maps, check the soils, and then he'll wonder if that's the optimum flow. He doesn't plop in his floatie until he knows the river will add value. Hansel is an optimizer, a disrupter, someone who believes anything can be improved. Things that aren't efficient bug the crap out of him. After 20 years of running marathons and ultra-marathons, he's trying to change the way he walks, so he can improve his running form. Even walking can be improved. You tell him the sky is blue, and he might tell you it's actually more of a cerulean blue today, and then google why that might be to find out more. That's how Hansel's built.

Nobody's faking any orgasms, but like Harry and Sally, Hansel and Wayne found a way to work well together, despite how they approach challenges so differently. Hansel is the company's founder and creator. Coding tools, logos and websites, processes and procedures, that's Hansel's job – to build and create. Helping franchisees use and understand these tools and procedures, giving them advice on running schools, and pulling experience from our own schools and franchisees everywhere, that's Wayne's job – to support and help execute.

In a franchisor business, both sides of the coin are equally important. Someone needs to create and implement the tools and processes that make up a company – without them, there is no company. But also, someone needs to roll those things out and support their users. In fact, that support is the very "product" that a franchisor company sells – a franchisee expects us to support them with our proven tools and processes. That, along with the original playbook and assets, is what the royalties are paying for.

With all the proprietary tools in our system (and there's a *lot*), Hansel builds it himself because he's pretty fast and can design it on the fly as he codes and iterates himself. A one-man team has downsides no doubt – but it's fast. When he's done, Wayne tests a bit more and gives feedback – basically acting like a user to make sure it works. The button shouldn't be there, the field doesn't accept apostrophes, whatever. And that's it – after that, we roll it out – sha-BOOM! Once it's rolled out, Wayne takes over as the support guy who helps our franchisees use the tools. That's about the most compact lifecycle you can have, and it's what makes us so agile and so well-suited to build new things for the company.

While our in-house software may have minor imperfections or missing features compared to commercial products, our agile approach allows us to address issues or add functionality uber-fast, sometimes within minutes. Our user pool is small (just our franchisees), and it's rarely mission-critical software, so that makes this style better for us. Facebook has been known to use this method, too – their motto at one point was "Move fast, break things." They would make constant changes and roll them out, but also quickly make updates and fixes as they go. But most companies still have a dedicated test team with coordinated rollouts, meaning they're more careful with testing something before rolling it out. A little more stability at the expense of a lot of agility.

This process not only works for us for building software, but it's also a microcosm of how our Yin has meshed with the Yang in our company roles – Hansel creates it, and Wayne supports it. Wayne's personality works great with supporting franchisees – he rolls with the punches, is easy-going, and patiently steers them in the right direction. Need a callback? Sure. How do I use this system? Wayne's gotchu. Supporting them is our product, and Wayne knows how to execute it well. Hansel's not as patient – he's probably more likely to just code an AI to answer all the calls and piss everyone off, but he'll come up with a process to get it done fast.

On the flip side, when a process isn't efficient, Wayne might be blind to it. "If it ain't broke, don't fix it" is Wayne's battle cry. He could spend all night collating data row by row and be absolutely fine with it. Hansel though, would be annoyed as hell and find some process to do it in an hour. It's the opposite thinking, but in our company, the Yin meshes perfectly with the Yang, and both sides are important. And in about 20 years from now, we fully expect to shoot a video on the couch about how awesome our marriage, a.k.a. theCoderSchool, has been. No kisses, but maybe a guest appearance by Meg Ryan and Billy Crystal AI bots.

Home Life

How we've evolved with tCS in large part stems from our home and family lives. We both have school-aged kids and love spending time with them (even if they're old enough now to not want to spend the time back). We both have wives who know how to keep us in check and support us, too, without whom neither of us would be where we are today, and both of whom we bounce lots of business ideas off of.

The Lynns in Orlando – we didn't go to any parks, too expensive

Hansel lives in Palo Alto with three kids and his wife, Lisa. Lisa is Hansel's "lobster" (as they would say in *Friends*), his first ever and only girlfriend who ended up being his

125

wife – kinda like a cool romantic movie. She's a Bay Area native, born there, high school in Mountain View, and even went to Stanford nearby. She'll say her involvement in oil painting over 8-9 years helped get her into Stanford. Yeah, right. That would get laughed out of the room in today's ridiculously competitive college applications.

Lisa grew up in an upper-middle class family – but they were all cheap as hell, and Lisa still is. As a family of 5, Hansel's family often eats $5 meals at home ($2 pack of tofu, $2 broccoli, and probably 20 cents worth of white rice), and $20 meals when "eating out" at Panda Express (the trick is to make your own rice at home and bring that coupon!). You'll often find Lisa in the Customer Service line at Target trying to get a price match just to save $2.

This frugalness definitely rubbed off on Hansel, who used to buy mountain bikes that cost more than cars – now he wears $10 t-shirts that last for 15 years. It's affected the money decisions at tCS, too – whether it's not paying for office rent or saving on travel meals, there's something incredibly satisfying about doing something super cheap. It feels so… efficient. That's not to say the family is cheap on everything – Lisa is a part-time house spouse (she coined that term – look for it to blow up) and a part-time real estate developer. Real estate definitely doesn't come cheap around these parts, but at least it's an investment, so the money doesn't just get pooped out like it would after an expensive restaurant. Very inefficient, as Hansel would say.

The Tengs at Velika Planina in Slovenia, one of Winnie's many planned trips.

Wayne lives in San Mateo, about 20 minutes north of Palo Alto, with his two girls and wife, Winnie. Winnie's the kind of person who loves the good travel deals. Not in a cheap way like Lisa, but in an efficient way, like finding the killer deal to fly to Spain with the kids or Abu Dhabi with her girlfriends. She's a travel nerd, and just like Wayne goes along with Hansel's tCS ideas, he and his girls follow wherever Winnie plans. She's a foodie, too, something that definitely didn't rub off on Wayne, who's more likely to pound the McNuggets with the kids when Winnie's away. For her day job, Winnie's an estate lawyer who started her own firm after having worked herself through both undergrad and law school (not an easy thing to do!). She and Wayne have that hard-work mentality in common, something Wayne locks in at theCoderSchool every day, and something they both hope will pass straight to their kids.

But really, the kids are the reason we do anything. Wayne's girls are just starting to become "real people," one going into high school and the other soon to follow. Both play tennis, the same sport Dad played for WashU's Division III team. Hansel's three kids are older, with two in college, one at NYU Shanghai and the other at WashU (just like Dad and Uncle Wayne) and one still in high school. They're self-sufficient now, which is a whole new stage of life for parents.

For you parents complaining about younger kids and needing to watch them all the time – stop your whining. You'll soon see, like we did, that there is no more amazing time in your life than when your kids actually want to spend time with you or when your child sees Disneyland or Hawaii for the first time and thinks it's the most magical place in the world. Cherish the time with your kids before they're off to college because it'll happen fast. And whatever you do, don't spend your time trying to make more money if it means you'll miss any time with them. Kids are the ultimate experience that will make you forget about making money. Nobody on their deathbed has ever regretted spending more time with their kids instead of working.

Outside of work, Hansel's a full-on introvert. The family doesn't do a lot of social events; they're just happy being at home with each other (even if the boys are often just on their phones). A rock-band lead singer and CEO of a community-based business is an introvert? Yep, it happens. Wayne's a bit more extroverted – in a social situation Hansel's energy might die out after a few hours, whereas Wayne can just keep the power on forever. It probably helps that Winnie is very social, and they do lots of social outings on the weekends with other parents and old friends.

While Wayne is more of a game-sport player like basketball or tennis ("exercise that's fun", as he calls it), Hansel's sport is the endurance stuff, like running, biking, or swimming and long races like Ironman. Not so much about the fun as much as it's about the suffering. Endurance sports push your body and mind into an uncomfortable zone, so you learn how to suffer in a controlled environment. This helps you become more comfortable with suffering when your environment isn't as much in your control. As Jensen Huang, CEO of Nvidia, said to a lecture hall full of Stanford students – "I wish you ample doses of pain and suffering." Resilience, he says, is the success factor in life that is born from our experiences in suffering. Whether you suffer by running 100 miles in the mountains for 28 hours, by doing all-nighters to roll out your minimum viable product, or by eating 30 White Castle sliders in a row – know that you'll be stronger for it. Unless you have a heart attack first.

A Day in theCoderSchool Life

We get together once a week to talk shop, meeting every Friday for a cheap lunch. Our meetings used to be at The Old Spaghetti Factory because they had all-you-can-eat soup and salad for like seven bucks. We'd focus on the soup and forget the salad because as the Asian families teach you – never eat salad at a buffet. The soup was clam chowder on Fridays, some of the creamiest clammiest goodness we've ever had. Hansel would use his endurance skills to plow through a gut full of chowder like he was running a half marathon. After a few years, the restaurant went out of business, which is probably all for the best, for us at least. Unlimited clam chowder every Friday for four years can take a toll on a restaurant business. And on a man. Our new favorite is Chick-fil-A down the street. Ever so slightly healthier – at least it's not all cream and carbs.

We tend to shoot the shit for the first hour of every meeting; asking about that recent family trip, whether we watched last night's Warriors game, or what we think of the latest news on AI. Then we get down to business and go down the enrollment numbers of every school. We used to go top-down, ending with the worst schools, but that bummed us out – so now we go bottom-up and it feels like we're rockin' by the end. Every month or two, we go "wow, that's actually pretty awesome." To see the average and total student count grow over time to where it is now is a special feeling. Something that came entirely from nothing – it's cool to see how far we've come.

During our review of each location's performance, we often pause to discuss specific schools in more detail, addressing different aspects of their operations. Sometimes it's random gossip ("Did you hear Claire Danes is one of the parents and came into the school?"), sometimes it's a recent status ("These guys sold the most camps ever!"), and sometimes it's down-to-

Visiting a school in Jersey

earth business ("They asked about opening their next location, does it *really* make sense or are they drinking the Kool-Aid?").

There are unfortunately usually a few laggard

schools that don't perform as well as we hope, and we try to come up with ideas to help them. Remind them of certain tools, help think of ways to do better marketing and try as best as we can to keep them accountable. In a franchise model, we can't do much for them directly – we can only guide and suggest, and hope for the best. That means it's up to the owner or manager, and sometimes, unfortunately, they don't have enough of the energy and desire that the school needs. People often ask us what we look for in our franchisees. The answer is that the best schools are the ones that have the passion and desire. We can support a school, but if they don't *really* want to do it, then they're not really going to do it.

On the flip side, we always like to stop when there's a school that's outperforming, or an owner that we really like that's doing well. We'll pause when someone's at an all-time high in student count, and we "ring the bell," a congratulatory announcement for locations that cross 100 students for the first time. We'll ring it again if/when they cross 200 and 300. Only one has crossed 300 which is crazy sauce, but that's the goal. There are more than a few owners that we really like as people who are just knocking it out of the park. Looking at their numbers are the feel-good moments, the times that validate why we love what we're doing.

Finally, we move on to random topics that we might have on the list. What's the status on the franchisor convention? How's this new college partnership thing turning out? This part of the meeting is a perfect microcosm of how our Yin fits with the Yang

Wayne might casually mention that kids love getting prizes, which then turns into two hours of Hansel brainstorming some crazy automated way to get kids prizes every month with Wayne chiming in to support every step of the way.

Hansel: "What if we picked the best app of the month and gave out a prize?"

Wayne: "Yeah, that'd be awesome!"

Hansel: "How about we let the kids access the database directly?"

Wayne: "Hell yeah, that'd totally work! Maybe!!"

Hansel: "Then I'll build an AI voting interface for the owners!"

Wayne: "Everybody would use it!!"

And so it goes, Hansel throws out some crazy idea that has a 50/50 chance of working, and Wayne is cheerleading the heck out of the idea, which sets Hansel off to throw out some more stuff. By the end of the meeting, either Hansel dang near designed the whole thing already or we've wasted two hours on something that made no sense in the first place, and we've dropped it. This dynamic of the brainstormer and the booster makes us more effective and is how most of the school was built. That's because without Hansel, there aren't the good (and bad) ideas and the ability to execute them quickly. Without Wayne, the ideas just die out without the momentum to keep going. Yin, meet Yang. Then spin in a perpetual circle.

Square Pegs and Round Holes

Even if we're working in perfect unison now, it wasn't always that way. Even Yin and Yang started off as just two semi-circles sitting opposite each other until they started spinning together. Similarly, the early years of theCoderSchool presented some big challenges in our working relationship. In the first three years of tCS, Hansel wasn't completely happy. He was pretty frustrated for much of those three years in fact, specifically about Wayne. In the beginning, there was no company yet, and as the story goes, Hansel invited Wayne aboard to help build it. But what Hansel didn't realize at the time was founding and building a company wasn't part of Wayne's toolkit. It was like trying to fit a square peg into the proverbial round hole.

Imagine the analogy of a company's growth as slashing your way through the jungle. Executors chop through the vines and brush to keep the company moving through the unknown. Leaders climb a tree to see which way they should chop. Hansel felt like he was chopping through the jungle and climbing trees but turning around to see Wayne staying behind to clean up the branches and cheering, "Let's go, H!" Hansel kept trying to get Wayne to help chop, but he would eventually just go back to gathering branches, all while happily cheering on Hansel.

It got to the point where Hansel seriously thought about letting Wayne go, actually firing Wayne because he wasn't able to help build tCS. It's a strange thing to write, given where we're at now. But for three years, Hansel wondered whether he should replace Wayne. But when you're in a marriage, you do what you can to make things work. If Wayne hadn't been the best friend, if the company hadn't been doing well, or if Hansel had wanted to grow faster – the honest truth is, Wayne might not be at the company today and this book wouldn't exist.

At one of our Old Spaghetti Factory meetings, three years in, things finally changed. Over a bowl of clam chowder, Hansel brought up the issue to Wayne again, and this time, Wayne said, "You know what, I'm just not built that way." He said that he worked differently, that he was more like a "machine," staying up late and knocking out whatever tasks he was given. The thing was, in the first three years of a company, being a machine is not enough. Machines don't run themselves – they need instructions to run. New start-up companies need machines, sure, but even more so, they need *programmers* to create the instructions for the machines.

Nevertheless, Wayne's comment was cathartic for Hansel. He finally realized that Wayne was right – that's just who he was. In fact, it's how Wayne had always been -- with the Asian parties, with Timmy Ramen, with Fantasy TeeVee – he's a doer who goes with the flow, not a builder and disruptor – so why would he be any different now? In many ways, Hansel felt he was at fault for bringing in Wayne so early and expecting him to do something that he knew deep-down wasn't a fit for Wayne. But the realization that Wayne *was* a machine and not a disrupter brought a new perspective – why not just find a differently-shaped hole to put the square peg?

Using the jungle analogy, Hansel realized that three years in, it wasn't just about moving forward anymore – we had to watch our backs, too. That's because after chopping jungle for a while, zombies might start coming at us from behind (bear with us here). At first, we'd both stop what we were doing and nunchuck 'em together. But as Wayne found his flow, he started knocking 'em out all on his own. Which then freed Hansel up to keep chopping jungle and forging ahead. We had figured out how to get through the zombie jungle together.

When the clam-chowder epiphany happened, the company was at an inflection point. Hansel had built much of the company already (he had cleared the figurative jungle path), and the next phase was more about support and working with franchisees – Wayne's wheelhouse. So, from that bowl of clam chowder on, Hansel's frustration subsided. While Wayne was not a founder that chopped through jungles, he became the zombie-shooter – the support – and by then there was plenty of supporting to be done. Despite some initial rockiness, we eventually figured out how to work together, and the Yin started to spin in unison with the Yang. We each were playing the role that fit perfectly with our personalities.

Looking back, this might have been the ideal partnership all along, even in those first three years. If Hansel had brought in another disrupter, would those years have been nearly as fun? Definitely not. tCS might have become a bigger company or be making more money, or maybe it might have even failed. But the life-experience philosophy now would likely be completely different. The times we had together, zombies and all, led us to the amazing times we're having today.

Part 3

The Adventures
of theCoderBros

Chapter 12

The Franchisee Family

Like Harold and Kumar, we've had our fair share of adventure stories on our way to finding our proverbial White Castle. Some of our favorite stories involve our franchisees, the same folks we call our family. Franchisees are our lifeblood, they not only make up who we are as a system, they help us grow, too, as a business and as people.

Our franchisees come in all shapes and sizes – technical ones, non-technical ones, those with entrepreneurial experience, and those who have never run a business in their lives. Men and women with all kinds of backgrounds from all over the country, some with large families of their own and some single without kids. The one thing they have in common is they're all good people. We're not here to pull one over on anybody or put anyone down – we're teammates. We're here to legitimately help each other and inspire each other. For us, those are the qualities that make a good franchisee. A franchisee needs to be someone we'd enjoy having a beer with, and thankfully, we enjoy having beers with good people.

Chinesing The Bill

We've personally been to most of our Grand Openings, especially the ones in a new city. Depending on our flight schedules, we may stay to celebrate with our owners after the opening. At one opening, our franchisees chose an upscale restaurant. Like a *really* upscale restaurant. We showed up in our standard hoodies and jeans to a dimly lit restaurant. You know, the type where they dim the lights on purpose to be extra fancy (after all, everyone looks better when the lights are low). Our franchisees showed up shortly after, dressed like they were going to a formal prom or something.

In any Asian culture, there's a lot of fighting for the check at the end of the meal. Never let the other party pay for the bill, or you lose face. In Cantonese, it's called "Haak Hei," meaning polite as all get-out. These franchisees were a group of Asian owners who were about the most generous people you could ever meet, so considering how nice the restaurant was and how well they dressed, we knew there was going to be a showdown-melee for the bill.

We took the opening salvo. Before the franchisees even got there, Hansel let the wait staff know that we would be paying the bill. Once we sat down and ordered, the franchisees took their shot, telling the waitress that they were paying and to give them the bill at the end. As Asians do, we all verbally fought over who would pay throughout the entire meal, with us finally relenting and saying ok – mostly to change the conversation. At the end of the meal, the franchisees asked for the check, but there wasn't one coming. That's because Hansel had used the oldest Hong Kong trick in the book by excusing himself during the meal to go to the restroom, but instead went to pay the check. "We WIN!" said Hansel.

As Bruce Lee probably once said, "Never trust your opponent when they say they need to pee." But alas, we were the losers in the end. When we got back home, we had a $1,000 Amazon gift card waiting for us (like we said, it wasn't a cheap meal). Considering that the night before, our dinner likely cost $25 at some fast-casual joint, it's pretty funny to see what kind of bill we were fighting for with our franchisees. For all the comical back-and-forth between us, it's this feeling of being generous to each other that we really appreciate.

The morning after the upscale restaurant, wearing OSU hats the owners gave us

And it's not just these folks, other franchisees are generous, too. One franchisee ditched our dinner for almost an hour while he stood in line in the bitter cold to buy us locally famous fudge as a gift. Another offered a room in their house to stay when we came to their opening (weird – but generous). Another gave

3D print of the Bruce!

us fragrant candles, which got us busted in the TSA line and almost made us miss our flight (mental note, wax doesn't show well on the x-ray machine). Still another sent each of us a giant 7-foot box of cookies during the Christmas season. The most meaningful gift was a 3D-printed Bruce Lee statue – over a foot tall, spray painted and made up of 17 pieces – that a manager (not even a franchise owner) made and gave to us. It's this kind of culture that permeates the system and inspires everyone to be better and to be there for each other.

Center of Sports

If you know where ESPN is headquartered, you can guess which tCS this next franchisee owns. The husband of this husband-and-wife team works at ESPN for his day job and was awesome enough to get us in for a tour. For sports fans like us, it was amazing to see where all the work was done. Since they weren't filming at the time, he was able to bring us into the studios. These were the actual studios you'd see on TV, where they filmed the NFL morning show and even the flagship show that made ESPN famous – SportsCenter. If you've ever seen this iconic sports news show, you'll recognize that giant desk that heavyweights like Chris Berman, Scott Van Pelt, or the late-great Stuart Scott sat behind at some point

Going live in 3... 2,,.

in sports history. And now, heavyweights like Wayne and Hansel have sat there, too, and we have the cheesy pictures to prove it.

Being the sports-celebrity nerds that we are, we were on the lookout for anyone famous. Alas, since it was Saturday, we didn't run into either Rich Eisen or Troy Aikman – but we did see Sage Steele getting ready for her show in her studio. We also got to see some of the places where they filmed ESPN commercials. It was awesome to be in the same hallway where Peyton and Eli were giving each other wet willies. We ended the tour by playing a few games on the Oculus, which was a brand-new toy at the time and not yet owned by Meta. As a bonus, with ESPN being owned by Disney, the franchisees shared a huge company discount with us for Disney World. When you get a discount to go see the Mouse, you feel like you're in more than just a business relationship. It starts to feel like a friendship.

This culture of friendship, if we're being honest, isn't something every company should have. Friends don't always make the best employers (or franchisors) because businesses can be brutal at times when profits come first. But for us, profits don't come first – finding the nearest thing to a win-win does. It doesn't mean that everybody always wins (that's not possible in the real world), but it does mean we try to think carefully about what's right for both sides before we think about our profits. While it's hard to get a diverse group of franchisees to all feel this way, we think many of them do. It's not a culture that can be dictated though; it has to be bred from within.

For example, we've always done our best to negotiate *against* ourselves. That's not common advice you'd get about negotiating, but we believe in it at tCS. One example is we give franchisees an automatically protected territory for their first 6 months to a year because we don't think it's right for another party to compete against them. It's not written anywhere, and no one asks for it, but for the good of everyone, it feels right to give it. We also give a grace period of up to two months before taking royalties, again, not because anyone asked but because we feel it's the right way to get them started. We've even refunded thousands of dollars of deposit towards opening future schools (through an Area Development Agreement) when an owner decided not to open more schools. You can bet that the agreement is legally air-tight and that deposit is legally non-refundable – but is refunding the right thing to do? We think so, and we think that reflects our culture.

That's not to say we give everything away or that it's chaos everywhere. We do enforce *some* rules, like the ones that affect the bigger-picture value of the brand. Safety is our most critical focus, and we allow no wiggle room. If a franchisee doesn't have the right background checks or forgets some safety quizzes – they're locked out of the system, no exceptions. We always tell folks upfront that we are very serious on safety, and that is one reason for which we wouldn't hesitate to terminate a franchisee and take over their location. And that's all a part of the culture because it's for the good of everyone, and our franchise family understands that (and are all diligent with their safety!).

Sometimes people see working with a partner or client as a zero-sum game, but it really isn't. All you need to do is think about both of your interests together instead of just yours, and you'll see that the sum is greater than the parts.

Fight City

Between the two of us, we've gotten in exactly zero fights in our lives. Not only because we're engineer weaklings, but also because we're both much more likely to back off than to engage with someone. But we've learned that not everybody is built that way, even if they're the nicest, coolest people otherwise. While our franchisees are all generally good people, occasionally we encounter situations that remind us of the diverse backgrounds and experiences our franchisees bring to the table.

It was a perfect, warm evening, the kind where you could wear shorts and a t-shirt outside and have a beer with friends. We had just attended a grand opening and decided to go out with the owners to a brewhouse with outdoor seating to celebrate. The two franchisees went back in to get us some drinks, but only one came out. When we asked where the other guy was, he calmly replied "I think he's getting in a fight." Turns out someone

Susheel and Sean who, let's be honest, were two of our favorites

made some offhand racist remark, and those became fightin' words. Luckily, it was just some chest puffery and stare downs, but the fact that it seemed so commonplace and they were so nonchalant about it was a little unsettling to us. These guys were people of color, and the truth is that the world isn't what it should be. The rest of the evening went off without a hitch, and this was a relatively minor incident, but it reminded us that people aren't all treated the same way, despite all the progress that we've made as a human race.

In our business, we want to treat everyone the same way, too. We may naturally have some folks we like more than others but treating all franchisees the same helps reinforce that family culture. Families don't work as well when one member always gets first dibs or another one always gets called out.

We once got a complaint from one of our franchisees that we had shown favoritism toward someone close to us and protected them more than we would have someone else. While we're glad that they felt honest and comfortable enough to bring up the complaint, it ended up being a miscommunication. But that complaint reminded us how important it was to not just treat everyone the same but to make everyone *feel* like they're being treated the same. Paraphrasing Maya Angelou here – it's all about how they *feel* that sets the tone.

Down South

"Scary Owner" Jerry (and family) plays nice

One of our favorite owners is this big, scary, black dude. No racism here, the dude is just a big, scary dude, and he happens to be African American. Facts. He talks in this low baritone, like James Earl Jones (RIP) in that super laid-back way like he's lulling you to sleep. That is, until one of his school's grand openings comes around. He'd start chest bumping us – "It's GAME TIME!" he'd yell because he used to play football back in college. We felt just as ready to tackle a parent to the ground as we were to explain our Code Coaching. But get to know this guy and his family, and you'll find he's not only a softie, but also has a great sense of humor that's right up our alley (lots of race jokes that shall never be published). And he's one of those guys who is always learning and trying to get better.

He's one of our owners who kept his full-time day job, and now owns four successful schools. That in itself is an uncommon feat. While he did find a great manager to help, he has also spent countless hours coming up with inventive new ways to serve his clients – YouTube camps, attention-grabbing marketing emails, Nintendo Switch tournaments. This owner knows how to think out of the box. Because he spends his time learning and improving, he's now probably our system's foremost expert on digital ads despite never having run one before his first tCS. All this while still getting promotions and raises at his day job, working his way up through upper management. *Scary Owner* (surely that nickname will stick, right?) proves that you can be wildly successful at multiple things at the same time, as long as you work hard at purposefully improving yourself and your business.

We Hate Politics

It was May of 2018, right in the middle of the Trump years, and midterm elections were right around the corner. On one of our calls with a school owner in Southern California, the owner said "Oh, we might be getting Ivanka Trump to come to our school." Say WHAT now? This was early on in our system, and we were only about 2 years old as a franchise with maybe 15-18 locations. Anyone more famous than the local school principal would have been a huge win at that point, much less the daughter of the President of the United States. Then the franchisee added, "Oh, this guy Kevin McCarthy might come, too." WHAT? McCarthy wasn't quite as well-known at that time, but he eventually became the Speaker of the House, otherwise known as third in line to the Presidency.

It turned out that the owner had a friend from college who was running for State Senator and had plenty of connections, including some to the White House. Also at that time, Ivanka was pushing for kids STEM and Computer Science and doing a tour around the country to meet folks like Hadi Partovi, the founder of code.org, a giant non-profit organization dedicated to kids coding.

Because these celebrity visits often fall apart, we were pretty sure it wasn't going to happen, so Hansel went to Hawaii as he had planned, and Wayne did his normal summer routine. Then we got the call – the franchisee had just gotten off the phone with the White House, and they were coming. It was part of a fundraiser tour for McCarthy; they had three stops planned, and theCoderSchool was the third. Hansel immediately paid for a $1,000 flight to get back from Hawaii the next day, and Wayne started brushing up on his Trump trivia and rehearsing "You're Fired!" in the mirror. Meanwhile, the franchisee started going through the secret service plan with us, telling us which alley they'd drive in, and how they would use the next store over as a staging area. It was exciting and crazy at the same time.

In the end, to no one's surprise, they had a last-minute cancellation. Still, it was a surreal possibility that it might have happened. Someone of that level of fame, that high up in our government, was that close to visiting one of our schools. Huge props to the franchisee who got it to that point. That in itself was a huge accomplishment. Once it set in that it wasn't going to happen and we talked about it a bit, we ended up letting out a huge sigh of relief. The Trump name was, and is, a divisive one. Although Ivanka Trump has a huge celebrity name, it would have been a risky visit because of the divisive politics of the time. As excited as we were at the start, the more we thought about it, the more it seemed like we dodged a huge political bullet.

The First Big Game

There was a time when we were NBA big-game virgins. Way back in our first year of franchising in 2016 (way before the even bigger game from the start of this book) we decided we wanted to celebrate our initial success. And we would celebrate it with our OG franchisee, Christian. He was the guy who gave us the idea to franchise in the first place, and that was the origin-story event that allowed theCoderSchool to become the company it is today. If anyone was deserving of a big ticket to the NBA Finals, it was Christian.

In 2016, Steph looked like he was 20 years old, but Lebron looked the same

That year, the Warriors were considered one of the best basketball teams in history, having won more games in the regular season than even our beloved Michael Jordan's Bulls from the 90s. With splash brothers Klay Thompson and Steph Curry, they easily made it to the Finals and matched up against the underdog Cavaliers. At the time, we had never been to a big NBA basketball game before, so we decided to celebrate our move to franchising by splurging on tickets to Game 5 of the NBA Finals, held at Oracle Arena in Oakland.

"Splurging" might be quite the understatement because the tickets cost $7,000. Each. And, we bought three of them because Christian came along, too. We thought we were gaming the system because c'mon, who wants three tickets? It must be cheaper than two tickets. Pretty stupid assumption on hindsight. But we were all-in and ready to take our first big shot at paying ourselves through experiences. We figured that 10 years from then, surely we wouldn't notice $21k less in the business bank account – so why not expense it to the company for a once-in-a-lifetime experience?

We sat in Row 1, which was right off the hardwood floor, behind one of the baskets. We now know from this book's Introduction that there's also rows AA and BB which are literally on the court, but at the time, damn those Row 1 seats were insane. Christian looked at us and said, "Dudes, how successful *IS* this business, anyway??" A little fake-it-till-you-make-it (at least at that time) goes a long way.

We got to the game maybe an hour and half early to check out the scene. Along with the tickets came access to a lounge, something we didn't even know existed until we chatted with the super-friendly security guard. To get to the lounge, you had to walk down a long tunnel. At the end of the tunnel was, literally, the player's locker room, where we of course couldn't go, but after a quick right turn, we were in the VIP lounge. The lounge was first class with a big ice sculpture that said NBA Finals 2016, surrounded by huge king crab legs and shrimp on ice along with other premium eats like sushi and prime rib. Never having been in a lounge like this, Christian looked at us and said "Uh, do we have to pay?" We had no idea, we'd never been in a lounge like this either. We felt too stupid to ask anyone, so we just walked back out and tried to play it cool, like we weren't hungry anyway. We all should have been kicked out of the Asian race for not taking full advantage of that buffet, which we found out later was of course included in the price of the ticket.

A few minutes later, the buffet was the furthest thing from our minds. As we walked back through the long tunnel, a security guard yelled at us to stop and move to the side. We stopped to turn and see what was going on, and just as we did, Mo Speights, their backup center, came running by us. We were in the player tunnel! After that, we figured out the secret – keep walking back and forth from our seats to the lounge, hoping we'd get stopped again and a player would come running past us.

Christian hangs with theCoderBros in the player tunnel where we found Steph

On our third try, we struck solid gold – Steph Curry, the greatest shooter to ever play the game, not only came running out, he stopped 2 feet away from us and bent down to tie his shoes. While Christian was busy pulling out the phone for a pic, Wayne slapped Curry on the shoulder and screamed "Let's GO Steph!!!" Hansel just stood there paralyzed, eventually repeating "What just happened, what just happened?!?" like a broken record. That kind of thing can't happen anymore because the new stadium, Chase Center, smartly separates the fans from the player tunnel. That up-close moment with Steph Curry was worth the entire free steak, shrimp, and crab legs buffet that we missed.

The game itself was awesome. The Warriors lost, but still – what a night. Lots of drinks, high fives, and yelling at the top of our lungs. After the game, as we sat there soaking in the moment, Tony Robbins walked by us. Maybe a little buzzed, Hansel screams "Hey Tony, you're awesome!" or something stupid like that as Robbins was walking away. To our surprise, he turned around and stared straight at Hansel. Robbins has those laser eyes that somehow make you feel an instant connection – as the world's leading life coach, he has that uncanny magical power.

Robbins walked right over, held his hand out warmly and said "Hey, I'm Tony. What's your name?" and shook hands with all three of us. In the middle of a wild stadium with loud fans everywhere, it was an amazing, almost intimate interaction. Although it was a fleeting introduction, we wouldn't be surprised if he remembered our names 10 years later – that's who Tony Robbins is. He made us feel important in that moment – and how you feel, as we (and Maya Angelou) have said, is the most important thing. Robbins had taught us an important lesson without even trying.

It was our first big splurge, an experience that we'll remember and reminisce about when we're old and retired. We would probably laugh about how we gave a $7000 ticket to Christian, who had opened our Seattle location that failed, and we'd think "should we *really* have brought Christian with us?!?" But it was

Christian that gave us that Bruce Wayne, dark alley, robbery-gone-wrong moment, that origin event in time that eventually made theCoderSchool. Christian was the first of our Franchisee Family, and while he didn't knock it out of the park on his location, he had a bigger impact on our company than anyone else (so a hearty THANKS if you're reading this, Christian!).

Chapter 13

Next Man Up

The General Manager (GM) position at our schools is a tough position. Not only do they need to act as the face of our school and take care of all operations, but they also need to sell to parents during the trial lessons, do marketing out and about town, and yes, know at least enough about technology to be dangerous. In short, they do it all. Sometimes the franchise owner fills that role, and sometimes they hire a GM. Even with all the responsibility and endless to-do lists, it's a rewarding job. GMs are the ones tasked with growing the school, and they are the ones who are rewarded with knowing that they are impacting kids throughout their community.

Aside from franchising, our company still owns and operates three locations – Palo Alto, San Mateo, and Cupertino, all in the San Francisco Bay Area. Operating these locations is a separate side of our business, one that Wayne focuses more on. He plays the same role that an owner would play if they hired someone – he manages the managers. As of this writing, we have three great GMs working with us. Will they be with us by the time you're reading this book? We hope so, but honestly, they may not. That's because GMs can be a transitional role, and we've rotated through a lot of them. In fact, even while editing this chapter, one just gave notice. We told you we know how this business works.

You have to have a PEZ dispenser kind of mentality when there's an important role like this that isn't always stable, so we operate around the Next Man Up philosophy. In the same way the backup quarterback might step in to play out the season if the main guy gets injured, Wayne identifies someone at each location that could become the next manager, should the current manager suddenly leave. True to that philosophy, all our current managers were a coach first before becoming that Next Man Up.

Like franchisees, the GMs across all the schools also come in all shapes and sizes. Some GMs like to coach a lot, others like to manage the coaches. Some work directly with parents, others delegate that responsibility. We have a younger GM who's a hardcore coder and can teach the most complex languages like Assembly. We also have one that came from sales but learned coding through a coding bootcamp. One on the East Coast currently has a job as a public-school teacher but still manages two schools. A few are younger folks who were fitness instructors, and a few are older folks who are grandparents. There's a long-time GM that started working for a location after retiring from a high-level executive position at a large bank, and another after retiring as an executive from a software company. The point is there is no "template" for what makes a good General Manager. Their backgrounds are diverse, but one thing they have in common is that they're there for the kids. Like many small businesses, we can't pay big corporate salaries. But if it's passion and emotional reward they're looking for, a coding school is not a bad place to find it.

Luckily for us (we're knocking on a lot of wood here), we're currently in the longest stretch of stable GMs we've ever had, even if one did just recently quit. But as you can guess, it wasn't always that way. Wayne's enjoyed working with all our GMs in different ways – but they certainly come with some quirks. They're all good folks, but to make sure we're sensitive to the way we're telling the stories, we've used fictional names in this chapter.

Doc Brown

Doc Brown was an original coach from back in the old days. He was an amazing coach, really excited to teach kids to code and really smart technically, too. He'd write these page-long notes to the parents telling them about what the student worked on that day – how the student felt, what concepts they worked on, even an explanation of some of the code. It was like a passion bomb blew up in your face when you read his notes. From an efficiency point of view, it was nuts – not only did it take a long time to write, but honestly it was so long we weren't sure parents would even read the notes. But that was the magic. Whether anyone read everything Doc wrote was almost beside the point – he had an amazing amount of passion, and that's what showed through. And like so many things, it wasn't the content of what he wrote, but how those notes made the parents *feel* about the lessons. The kids were being taken care of by a coach that was clearly passionate about their kids.

Doc was so good at being a coach that we decided to promote him to GM. While rewarding someone for their work in one role with a promotion to another role is a common mistake at many companies, we didn't realize our mistake until a few years later. It's especially common to promote someone who's good at doing something because you assume they would be good at managing other doers – but it's often not the case. That's because the skillset of the tactical worker (the coder, the lawyer, the artist… i.e., the worker that does the work) is a completely different skillset than a manager. But promote we did, and Doc became the new face of our school.

In the beginning, we were killing it. Doc would have a huge smile on his face with his hands clasped together when talking to parents and excitedly say "OOOHHHH!!" and lead them over to the computer to show the kids something. The school grew organically to over 200 students, without much effort. We felt like Doc's reputation was spreading, and parents started telling other parents about our school and the passionate GM. Doc was coaching a lot, too. Sometimes he would coach so much that he barely had time to lift his head up. One time we walked into the school and the temperature was 90 degrees! Doc was so passionate and heads down that he sometimes forgot that he's also responsible for the rest of the school, including turning on the AC. Other than the sauna, the setup was working, the school was growing, and as we often like to say, we were ballin'.

Until we weren't. In a business like this, the good times don't last forever. As they say in the NFL, winning breeds laziness. We were winning, and we got lazy. When our schools are flying with hundreds of students, we're more relaxed than we should otherwise be with lead generation, sales, and everything else. This started impacting our numbers a little bit in 2019, although not to a point where we would yet be concerned – but then the pandemic hit. It came and went, and while we still survived better than most, like many businesses, we weren't thriving afterwards.

To get our numbers back up, it was all about marketing, sales, and running a tight ship. Unfortunately, Doc's strength is coaching. As much as we tried to guide him along and support him to raise our numbers, marketing and lead generation just wasn't something in his wheelhouse. We had been lucky with growth in the beginning, but growing the school post-pandemic with a GM who was more of a coach at heart was another matter. After 6-9 months, we made the hard decision to reduce the GM role for Doc, and eventually let him go.

It took a lot of conversations between the two of us, but in the end, it was Hansel's push to move on from Doc. Just like on the franchising side, we work to our strengths in operations, too. Wayne's personality was a perfect fit as a direct report for our GMs, rolling with the punches and directly supporting them. Hansel was a level removed, and from afar, tried to make sure the key indicator numbers were positive and processes were being followed. This meant that when it came to making tough moves, Wayne was sometimes too close to the action. He knew

Doc too well, liked him as a person, and kept fighting to keep him. But like professional sports, when you're not winning, a change needs to be made. Seeing our student numbers continue to plateau and even drop, Hansel made the tough call, and Wayne executed it. In sports, the first change made is usually the head coach – in this case our beloved GM, Doc Brown.

Jeff Spicoli

One of our coaches back in the day was an amaze-balls marketer. Spicoli was probably the best GM that we had ever met when it came to marketing. He didn't have a car; he just rode around on his bike from home to our school and then some. He had an electric bike, so he could get power up and down the hills around us like they were nothing. Like many of our GMs, he had started as a coach and was even a self-taught coder. As luck would have it, it wasn't long before an opening for the GM job came up, and with his ability to connect with people and his great marketing skills, he was thrown in with both feet into the GM position.

He grew that school to the highest it's ever been, and it's never gotten close since. We've always said that grassroots marketing, where you are handshaking and meeting people in person, has always been the best form of marketing for a business like ours. And Spicoli was the best. He would jump on his bike and go to all the elementary and middle schools around town and stop in to introduce himself. He would chat with principals, parents, robotics clubs, and teams – you name it, he was out promoting theCoderSchool with them.

He was also always thinking about new ways to improve the school. He'd move furniture around constantly, at one point even moving the heavy front reception desk into the middle of the big open lesson room. So he was a little eccentric, Wayne thought. But we didn't care. He easily blew the school up to over 200 kids, and we were stoked. He'd earned his liberties and could turn the furniture upside down for all we cared as long as he kept everyone happy and grew the school as well as he had.

As we said with Doc Brown, good times don't always last forever. We started to see some clues along the way. At first, it was innocuous. He would set up pizza and video game nights and play some games along with the kids – awesome. Then, we found out that sometimes he'd stick around to play the games himself after everyone left. Ok, but not a big deal. But then, we'd find out he'd play the games all night long and stay overnight in our school. Sometimes, Wayne would go into the school in the morning and see empty pizza boxes everywhere and find Spicoli asleep in the office. Eccentric or warning sign?

Suffice to say things got stranger from there, including finding out he was a medical marijuana user and that he had a crush on one of the staff. We'll leave the rest of the details to your imagination, but to no one's surprise we let Spicoli go. If you're *really* curious, give Wayne a call and he'll go over all the details with you over a beer!

Elle Woods

We'll get straight to the point – Elle was one of our best. A story that we're both proud of. Elle came to us long ago and applied for the position of front-desk coordinator. The front-desk position at our schools is an entry-level job, which typically starts with being a greeter to parents but usually advances to other day-to-day admin tasks, like scheduling and chatting with parents. At that point, Elle didn't have the most impressive technical background, as she was a nanny at the time and someone who had immigrated to the US from another country. Her English was fine – though she wasn't a native speaker.

She wanted to push her boundaries, so she learned to code Scratch well enough to teach some of our younger students. Scratch is a straightforward language, and we often tell our franchisees that any logical adult can learn it and teach kids with it – if they have the time and commitment to really learn it. Elle did, and shortly after, she moved from the front-desk role to a bona fide Code Coach. Because she was able to coach and help parents with things like scheduling and even reaching out to leads, in a lot of ways, she was putting herself in a position to become an Assistant GM. Seeing how well she was doing, Wayne had already pegged her as the Next Man (or, in this case, Woman) Up. And when the GM position at a nearby school opened up about a year later, she jumped on it and transferred to that school to be a full-fledged GM. Elle was moving up in the world and building her resumé, fast.

She was always appreciative of the opportunities that theCoderSchool gave her, even after she left us years later. While she was with us, she'd always tell us, without prompting, how she was enjoying her time, and was learning so much, and wasn't going anywhere. That she wasn't leaving us for another job was perhaps a subtle knock on the GMs before her or perhaps a brilliant strategy to influence us in continuing to promote her. If so, it worked. In addition to working on the Operations side as a GM, we started to use her on the Franchising side. She would support a franchisee here or there and join our training sessions so that she might eventually do the training for us.

Eventually, Hansel gave her an even bigger jump. He had recently decided to let our expensive Director of Sales go because it would be cheaper to bring franchise sales in-house. Nurturing franchise leads, after all, wasn't much more than a bunch of emails and phone calls – like we've said before, sales to us is just talking to people. So Elle, barely a GM, not many more years removed from moving to America and a job as a nanny, was given the title of Director of Franchise Development. The look on her face when Hansel slid the offer letter with the salary bump across the desk was priceless.

If we had a nickel for every time Elle told us she loved what she was doing and was going to stay with us for a really long time, well, then maybe we'd eat *two* Chick-fil-A sammies in one sitting. Nevertheless, after rotating through lots of GMs before her, Wayne didn't entirely trust that she would stay, and his gut was right. About six months after her promotion into franchise sales, Elle gave us the standard two-week notice. It was an amicable split, though; she got a dream job at a startup that she couldn't pass up. She took it, and we couldn't blame her – we congratulated her.

Lucy Van Pelt

Not all our GMs left amicably. We had a GM that got Wayne about as mad as Wayne gets, and that's pretty rare. Lucy was a fairly good GM at first – technical, good with parents, good all around. Like most of our GMs, she was also promoted from a Code Coach position. Like Elle, Lucy also had dreams of something bigger than being a GM.

Lucy's boyfriend at the time had recently launched an automotive-related startup and had developed a prototype vehicle for the venture. He needed some help for some upcoming presentation, and Lucy asked Wayne if she could take a hiatus of a few weeks to help her boyfriend. Wayne being Wayne, he was supportive. This sounded like a cool startup, so why not give Lucy the opportunity to get up and close to it in person? Wayne would team up with others on the staff to hold down the fort, something that would take quite a bit of work over the two weeks that Lucy would be gone. But Wayne was game – grinding out tasks was his thing.

Two weeks passed, and Lucy didn't come back. In fact, she asked for an extension. Ok, Wayne said, hesitantly. Two more weeks passed, and something was happening with the startup such that Lucy couldn't come back, yet. She was starting that game of pulling that football away from Charlie Brown. "What the hell," Wayne thought, but he let it slide and diligently kept the school plodding along. Finally, after a few more delays, when Lucy was due back come hell or high water, Wayne got the call. She wasn't coming back. She was going to take her shot at a startup with her boyfriend.

This was two months after she first left us, mind you. Wayne sent her an email and didn't hold back. He said it was unprofessional and told her how much her absence impacted the team. For Wayne, that was about as mad as he gets (he loves to swear for fun, but not when it's at someone). And for us both, Lucy's bridge was quickly burned. About a month later, she came crawling back to Wayne asking for her job back, saying something about her boyfriend's prototype car having been destroyed in a freak accident. Wayne didn't really care what happened to the car at that point (although it did sound like it could have been a good story). The only thing he could think was "Karma's a bitch, ain't it?" And then basically told her to fuck off.

Revolving Door

We've had many more GMs, unfortunately. A few who weren't technical at all, which caught up to them eventually when technical parents wanted to hear more. One who was *too* technical and wanted to automate everything about the job, so he didn't have to do the job. And one who fell for one of those gift-card scams and went to buy two $200 gift cards from Safeway to send to some unnamed emailer – thinking that Hansel was asking him to buy the gift cards for him. Go figure.

A few more that we haven't mentioned, but like we said, it can be a transitional job until you find the right person.

Our franchisees have the same problem – some locations are just rotating GMs until they find the right one. But a lucky few have found the most amazing GMs you could hope for, who appear to be a life-long member of theCoderSchool family. When that happens, it's like hitting the mother lode. Since day one, we've wanted to nail down the ideal profile for the role of being the face of one of our schools. Ten years later, we're no closer to finding a pattern. We now say that we have no idea whether that awesome GM will be technical or not, good at sales or good at marketing, whether they are a parent themselves or are a single dude. The only thing we know is that good GMs love their job, and they're hard as hell to find.

Chapter 14

Coaches and Kids

What sets our business apart from the other coding schools is our Code Coaches. We don't call them instructors, but rather they're "coaches" who guide the students along based on the child's strengths and needs. As of this writing, we have over 1,300 active Code Coaches in our system, all expert coders in their own way, and all passionate about helping the next generation. When you consider a top university like CalTech in Pasadena only has about 300 on their faculty, 1,300 Code Coaches feels like a pretty big number.

Like the A-Team of the 80's, each school aims to find a group of coaches that specialize in different things, whether it's certain languages or teaching a larger class vs a private lesson. Depending on the location, the staff could consist of a lot of college students as coaches, or just a few. We also hire a lot of adults who have graduated – sometimes they have a CS or related degree and other times they're self-taught coders. And we're always on the lookout for the coder pro, that guy or gal that's a professional coder in the real world that just wants to give back to the next generation and teach for a few hours a week. Most schools have 1-2 of these coder pros.

Our franchise system has hired thousands of coaches through the years, and we've met hundreds of them. We think of all of them as "quirky" (in a good way), because that kind of personality is often a great fit for kids. While we don't keep statistics on gender and race, anecdotally, we'd guess that at least half of our staff are those of color. As much as we always strive to have as many female coaches as possible to have better representation, the truth is they are generally harder to find. We estimate that 1/3 of our staff identifies as female – not bad, considering Google tells us somewhere around 20% of computer science degrees are earned by females (data as of 2016).

Whatever their background, they're all expert coders who have a certain level of patience and goofiness to effectively work with a kid. Ironically, it's usually not the hardcore coder you might find at a tech company like Facebook, but rather the good, solid coder who's also great at working with kids (and has the time to do it!).

Ted

All our coaches know how to code, but they aren't all coding geniuses like Ted was. He was also a high-energy, happy-go-lucky guy. Always had a smile on his face, and an ability to talk about any and everything technical or scientific under the sun, even though he never got a college degree. But he was so knowledgeable about so many things, you wouldn't blink an eye if we told you he was a tenured professor at Stanford.

Hanging with Coach Ted at an opening

He once told us that the reason he didn't get a degree, and even had a hard time in high school, is that he just isn't good at learning through curriculum. It was too limiting, and he never found his footing. He said, in fact, that there's a good number of kids out there like that, where the teaching style didn't accommodate the child. Ted was living proof that not doing well in high school doesn't mean you're not smart – it might just be the teaching style didn't fit. It was part of the reason he liked teaching with us so much; instead of following a curriculum, we teach by immersion, and coaches like Ted are free to teach in a way that works best for the student.

Ted was creative, too. Before every lesson, he would play 5 minutes of ping pong with a kid while they talked about what they would learn that day. Or he started a trend of getting kids to stand up and write out logic on the white board, so kids are forced to think through it instead of just running it on the computer. He's also a coach who would do pirouettes and pliés to show the kids how to spin and duck their online characters because Ted, believe it or not, was an accomplished ballerino before he became a Code Coach. He didn't look like a ballet dancer, but apparently, he had danced for most of his life and was still doing performances as an adult.

Ted was a keeper, but like most of them, he eventually moved on. After working with us for years, he finally left us for a good reason. He got his dream job – working as a software engineer at a tech company. It was a job he likely couldn't have gotten without a college degree, but being a Code Coach might have opened that door. Even then, he'd come back occasionally and teach on Saturdays. When we're used as a stepping stone to something better, we're more than happy for our staff to get what they deserve once they move on.

Other Coaches

Ted's brilliance in coding was rare, but we've had other pretty amazing coaches too. The cool thing is that we feel like we created this new marketplace, this place where people who could code but don't want to (or don't fit) into a corporate world could thrive. A place where they could not only show their chops but also impact the next generation. It's too much to talk about all of our coaches, but here are a few memorable personalities:

- Michael, who started in Palo Alto when we opened. He was the first one to start teaching crazy complex stuff to young kids (C# to early middle-schoolers, for you techies), and often kept Hansel around after hours just to talk about the latest coding theories. After leaving us to become a full-time CS teacher, Michael expressed how fulfilling his role as a Code Coach had been, describing his work at theCoderSchool as a source of daily motivation, or in his own words "it's what gets me out of bed every day."

- Skyyler, who was a transgender coach in Palo Alto that was well loved by all her students and parents. Ironically, she was also one of those coaches that never did the admin tasks (writing notes, doing student reviews, etc.), but she was so good at teaching, we let the admin stuff slide. She later left us to work on a cutting-edge tech startup as a CEO – not a bad next gig!

- Hannah, who was our best 5-star review generator in Cupertino. She was an older coach who was like everyone's grandma, giving kids hugs hello and genuinely caring about what they were learning. She was one of the first to really spend time talking with parents before and after her lessons, and really poured out that passion. We later found out her day job was the World Lebanese Cultural Union (WLCU) Ambassador to the United Nations!

- Deanna, who was so good at teaching kids in San Mateo that some of her students cried when she left. On the plus side, she left for a great full-time job, but sometimes it's hard for the kids because they've formed this tight relationship with their coach. Many of our coaches get thank-you cards and Christmas cards too – it's just a part of that kind of relationship.

- Steven, who was working at a pizza joint when he found us and applied for a job in Palo Alto. Coming from a pizza place, you wouldn't necessarily think he was the best coder. But this guy was a genius. He knew his physics and vectors, and of course, coding too. He's one of the many coaches we've had that are "quirky" because they either don't want to, or don't fit into, a 9-to-5 job. Instead, they go off finding that odd job, which, lucky for us, included becoming a Code Coach.

Laker

Our coaches may be quirky, but they've taught some pretty amazing kids. Laker was one of the first kids to walk into our first school in Palo Alto during our 2014 grand opening. Laker was a 6th grader at the time, but we could tell right away that he really wanted to learn to code. He would be there through our entire opening, trying to figure out the coding problem we gave him, and he never gave up. We knew from that day that this would be a special kid.

Laker was the friendliest kid, always had a smile, and always happy to tackle the toughest problems. He had no problem having full conversations with adults, too, a skill that kids his age often lack. His mom is also amazing, she became one of our power-parents, someone who advocated for us, and helped spread the word about us (thank you, Debbie!).

About a year later, Laker's coach (Steven, the coach who came from a pizza place) brought in a book on math vectors. Kids this age, they don't often read books about vectors. But Laker devoured it in one night in between his 7th-grade homework. Laker's progress from there was nothing short of amazing. He won our first Coder Fair with an app that included complex physics formulas and vectors that emulated black hole gravity. He went on to build other apps, including Minesweeper, the classic game that came with every PC in the 90s. After a few years, he grew beyond what we were able to teach him, so he stopped attending. He kept in touch though, one time asking if there was any software system he could code for us at tCS. After graduating high school, he went on to attend MIT, basically the top computer science university in the country. Was he accepted to MIT because of us? Maybe. Well, definitely not – but we're proud of him, nonetheless.

Hansel visited Laker at MIT when he was a freshman, as Laker was kind enough to offer a tour of the campus for Hansel's son Beck, who was evaluating colleges at the time. Laker told Hansel the secret to being accepted to MIT is to "apply sideways." If

Hansel with Laker at MIT

you Google "MIT Apply Sideways," you'll see an article by Chris Peterson, a director of admissions at MIT which goes into more detail. The long and short of it is not to do things just because you think it'll get you into MIT. For example, don't go and try to build a nuclear reactor in your garage just to look impressive (spoiler alert, that kid did not get into MIT). Instead, study hard, be nice, and pursue your passion – whether that passion is science, a sport, or an instrument. There's that word again, passion. Turns out MIT (all the top colleges, actually) looks for people who are passionate. That's not unlike what we aim for at every level of our company, whether franchisee, general manager, or coach. It's no secret that passion is the secret sauce to most things in life.

Laker was a great tour guide, showing us every aspect of MIT. We were even lucky enough to watch a chase scene being filmed right outside MIT for Casey Affleck and Matt Damon's new movie, *The Instigators*. At the end of the tour, Laker said something Hansel won't soon forget. He said that he wanted to do this for us because he wanted to pay it forward, and he encouraged Beck to do the same to someone else after he went to college, whether it would be at MIT or not (it would definitely *not* be because MIT is impossible to get into). When Laker was in high school, he said someone helped him out the same way, so this was his way of passing the good karma to the next batch of high schoolers.

There are smart kids and there are good kids, and Laker is both. We're proud to have been a small part of his growth story, and hope he remembers us when he goes off to change the world. A small shoutout for tCS will suffice when he accepts his Nobel Prize.

The Best of the Rest

Aside from Laker, we've had a lot of students. At this point, as a system, we've easily taught well over 100,000 of them. Our students tend to be on the younger side, anywhere from about 7 to 14 or so. They stay anywhere from about a year on average to 5 or 6 years on the high end. We do have a few really advanced kids who are up to 17 years old, but most kids that age tend to be too busy thinking about college and move on by then.

We once taught an 80-year-old man how to code – he said it was on his bucket list, so he came in and we taught him to build a website. We even once taught a kid who was blind. Because he couldn't see the monitor clearly, he had a braille keyboard with an audio screen reader. It was amazing to listen to the audio reader describe the screen in 100x speed speech. The coach couldn't understand a word of it because it was so fast, but the blind student soaked it all in. Seems some senses really do become heightened if you lose another. And we'll often get kids on the ADHD spectrum as students. Turns out, a lot of them gravitate to coding because it's an activity that they have full control over, and one that can have less distractions especially in a private lesson.

Like the best kung fu movies, many of our students eventually become the teacher. They stick around long enough that we invite them first to be an intern with us, then later a paid Code Coach. Or they move far away from home to go to college only to end up teaching at a tCS location across the country. One made an Instagram video about her time as a San Francisco student who later moved to New York City and became a Code Coach.

Another became his high school Class President and used his graduation speech to tell the story of how he helped a painfully shy student break out of his shell at theCoderSchool. His message to his classmates was whatever your job, find a way to help others. And that even in – or perhaps especially in – the internet age, there is no substitute for human interaction. His message spoke to the heart of who we are at theCoderSchool. We may be teaching technology, but we believe that direct human interaction is the best way to connect, whether it's learning to code or forming relationships with others.

Chapter 15

The Fear Factor

When you start a new business, it's all sunshine and rainbows. As you get bigger, you realize it's a numbers game and eventually unexpected shit hits the proverbial fan. The stories in this chapter might sound crazy, but they're stories many other retail businesses have as well. Like any business with lots of clients and staff (not to mention lots of independent franchisees) theCoderSchool can't control everything – but we do our best to have systems in place to prevent issues as best we can.

Issues like lawsuits and threats of them can scare the pants off you when it's your own business. Whether it's a formal complaint for unpaid hours, sexual harassment issues, or that outlier parent going way over the line, we've seen it all. If you're looking for some eye-opening stories about a kid's education business, then buckle your seat belts and put the Stephen King book down, this chapter is all you need to scare the bejezeezuz out of you.

Labor Laws

We've had a few run-ins with labor laws, which are tougher than most people realize, especially in California. Whether it's overtime, breaks, or unpaid wages, it can be hard to keep track of the right pay when you have over 50 hourly employees working for you, which we do in our three schools. We have never been seriously accused of labor violations in our schools. That's because we treat our employees like family, and when we make mistakes (which aren't uncommon, considering how complex labor laws are), we apologize and let them know upfront, and then we make it right immediately, even if it costs us extra. We treat them like the people they are, not dollar signs to be saved or employees to be used. When there's a good relationship, you're less likely to get lawsuits, and more likely to just get an inquisitive email.

Sometimes a franchisee however doesn't follow that guideline with their own employees. There has been at least one instance of a franchisee being sued for unpaid wages. The wages themselves weren't a lot, but the management had a less-than-friendly way of dealing with the employee and their unpaid wages. The result was a lawsuit which was eventually settled for a much larger amount than the unpaid wages in the first place. When lawyers get involved, dollars tend to automatically jump up.

We've also had some complaints in the system about another side of labor laws – discrimination and retaliation. One unhappy ex-worker filed a formal complaint with the EEOC (Equal Employment Opportunity Commission) that she was being discriminated against because she's black. The funny thing was, the person she accused of discrimination was also black. That case didn't go too far.

We ourselves had an informal complaint about retaliation because the staffer was let go after complaining about her immediate boss. What she didn't know is that professional retaliation, like getting fired because you are insubordinate to your boss, is totally legal and fine. What employers can't do is fire people because they accuse someone of discrimination for example, an entirely different kind of retaliation. Some acts are protected from retaliation (e.g., whistleblowing), and others are not (e.g., being a dick to your boss). It's a good thing we have good lawyers (and Google) to get us through all this.

Asshole Parents

In our formal training is a slide called Asshole Training that all coaches, staff, and franchisees are taught. The idea is we're a business that's open to the public, and it's a numbers game. 90% of parents out there are super nice and supportive, 9.9% of them are a little bothersome and helicopter parents, but only 0.1% or less are real assholes. We tell all our franchisees coming in that we hope they don't encounter one, but if they do, stay calm and think back to training. Because if you expect the possibility, you'll be much more mentally ready to react.

One time, we had a camp where one of the camp counselors, Jane (not her real name), was a younger girl, small in stature, maybe 5 feet tall. She was having trouble with one kid and his audio volume one day and had asked him to turn it down a number of times. She finally said, "Next time, I'm going to unplug that speaker".

The next day, the dad comes rushing in first thing in the morning, a big, tall dude, maybe over 6 feet tall. Jane happened to be there early by herself as campers filed in. The dad comes right up within a foot of Jane, towering over her, and just starts berating and yelling at her, pointing fingers and all. He says she threatened his son, his son was emotionally damaged, and he couldn't believe we would run a business by threatening children. This, folks, is what we call an "Asshole Parent". Threatening staff about not-threatening students, all over unplugging an audio speaker. Although she was physically scared, Jane didn't call the police. It's often hard to remember to dial 911 in a fast-moving situation, but we tell our staff to keep it in mind. If you need to, you need to – safety is the first priority.

In the end, Wayne apologized to the parent for the child feeling that way (being careful not to apologize for anything *we* did because we didn't do anything wrong), and just calmly told the parent we needed to part ways. A few refunds later, that was the last we saw of that parent. Thank goodness.

(Really) Abnormal Parents

In another city, one of our franchised schools had a trial lesson. Sometimes the parent sits next to the child during the trial and did so in this case. Our schools usually have an open concept with one larger open room, and this school was no different. During the trial, in this open room with other lessons happening all around, the parent proceeded to put his hand where it didn't belong. The coach just froze. Just didn't know what to do. She didn't slap the hand away, just tried to power through the lesson. No one around noticed, and no one said anything.

After the lesson, the coach went home very distraught and later told the franchisee, who then reported it to us. Our first priority was ensuring the coach felt safe to return, and after a while, she did, and we all appreciated it. Meanwhile, the offending parent asked the school when they could sign up! Of course, the franchisee refused, but it's disturbing that this crazy parent thought nothing of what happened and wanted to sign up. In a room full of other coaches and students, this parent decided to put his hand where it didn't belong. Perhaps it was a cultural difference (though that is a stretch), but there are parents out there who are definitely part of that small 0.1 or less percent of the population that don't exactly fit the normal parental mold.

We've since emphasized in our training that coaches should never be afraid to speak up if a client crosses a line, and that we should all look out for each other, and help support each other if another person acts inappropriately.

Insurance

As a Franchisor, you can get roped into any kind of lawsuit even when your franchisee does something unrelated to you. Insurance helps protect a company from all the horror stories you read in this chapter. In America, anyone can and will sue for anything, and it's up to us to protect ourselves.

To do that, we currently pay upwards of $40,000 a year for insurance. That's a lot of insurance, but it's also some peace of mind. It won't protect against the stress that comes with a lawsuit, but it'll protect the company from going under if someone comes at you with a lawsuit for $20M. If you do the simple math, it's a lot of money burned every year, considering we've never had to file a claim. Insurance is funny that way. On the one hand, you never want to file a claim; it would mean something bad has happened. On the other hand, you sort of want to file *something*, just to get your money's worth.

At School of Rock, Hansel had some extra insurance, something called Sexual and Physical Abuse and Molestation (SPAM) insurance. It's strongly recommended for all tCS locations, too. It's a part of our insurance that we'd *really* never want to use, but if you have to, it's worth every single penny. Long ago, it was something Hansel found out firsthand, something that only he can explain in his own words. Fair warning, the rest of this chapter gets a little dark, so feel free to skip it if you'd rather keep it light!

Rock Me Like a Hurricane: Hansel's POV

The most influential story for theCoderSchool, ironically, didn't happen there. Instead, it happened at School of Rock, a music school for kids, where I was a franchisee. At that time, tCS was about 3 years old, and I was running both businesses. I had just come back from a summer vacation in Thailand and got a voicemail from my SoR manager Felix. Felix was a happy-go-lucky guy, probably the best manager I've worked with because he was so passionate about music and willing to learn about business. The voicemail he left me said something like "uh, hey the police just came in, and they wanted a list of all our students 15 and older." What a fun way to wake up from jetlag.

As we tried to figure out why the police would need our student list, Felix got a call from one of our instructors, Jeremy (not his real name). It was a serious call, and Jeremy said that not only had he relapsed into drugs, but he had also called the suicide hotline. Mental health is a serious matter, and while we felt terrible for what he was going through, we said that we would do our best to be there for him – but we of course had to let him go, as he could not go on working for a children's business while dealing with drug issues. Little did we know that was the tip of the iceberg.

Jeremy had disconnected his phone right after he had contacted Felix and was, as far as we could tell, in the wind. Unbeknownst to Felix and me, the police were trying to find him. We were kept in the dark the entire time because the police would not offer up any information. What was the purpose of getting our student list? Why did they need to find Jeremy? They say people fear the unknown, and that's exactly what we felt.

Meanwhile, we had not shared our student list with the police for privacy reasons. That sounds sketchy looking back, but the police would not give us any information whatsoever and giving them the contact information for our current clients without any context seemed to go beyond a privacy line. In the end, the police got a search warrant anyway, so that contact list was shared. A relief for me actually, as it meant I was absolved from having to make a decision to share that list.

With the police now in possession of parental contact information, I felt obligated to preemptively reach out to these parents. I didn't want the police to call them without warning. I personally called each of the parents that were on the list (it was only for female students 15 and up, about 12 parents). Those were some tough calls to make. You just don't know how a parent will respond to something like that, and you just don't know what rumors might spread about your business because of it.

I remember the exact place in my house where I made these calls, and I can see myself doing it from a third-person perspective, like an out-of-body memory. But my mind completely blacked out who I called and what I said. Maybe too much stress does that to your brain. I do remember I went for about a three-hour run to clear my head after that.

After those calls, I knew I needed to email the rest of the parents of our entire student body. Imagine the feeling of trying to be transparent and informative on one hand, while on the other thinking you might destroy the entire business you built. I just kept thinking "there must be another way." From the outside, this hesitancy can sometimes be misinterpreted as being deceptive, but from the inside, there's a lot of swirling thoughts and stress that make you want to slow things down. But eventually, I did it.

About a week later, we read on nextdoor.com that Jeremy was arrested. If you thought the phone calls and emails to the parents were the shit hitting the fan, this is the shit bouncing off the fan blades and flying everywhere. The local media, satellite dish on top of their van and all, pulled up to our school and wanted quotes from the staff. They got my personal cell somehow and texted me for comment. My friends were telling me they saw my business on TV. It was a circus of bad news for School of Rock in Palo Alto.

All this local news meant another round of communications to parents, including any parent who had been with our school in the last year. Again, I want to emphasize that these are hard emails to write. You want to be cooperative and transparent, but every word you type feels like a dagger to the very business that you started yourself from white walls and concrete. I wanted to be that unselfish guy who cooperated for the good of everyone, with not a thought to my business. But that's just not as easy as it sounds when you're at ground zero. I did have a good relationship with almost every parent, and by and large they were all very supportive. That can't be said for all of them; some of whom I considered friends turned against me, accusing me of things that weren't true. I can't blame them because this is a sensitive subject that deals with their kids being exposed to this now-criminal, but at the time it was hurtful.

Throughout this, SoR corporate was very supportive, with a PR and investigative team to help. This was, of course, partially to defend themselves as well, but I much appreciated the help.

They were able to get in touch with the police directly and found out that they needed our student list because they were looking for Jeremy and had reason to believe that one of our students would know his whereabouts. This is where this story turns from one about drugs and an arrest to one that involves harming a minor.

It turned out that Jeremy was having a relationship with one of the students, a 15-year-old. This is what Jeremy was arrested for – "lewd and lascivious conduct" and that relationship with a minor. It was mind-blowing. It was heart-wrenching. It was under my watch, and there was nothing I could do. By then, Jeremy was in prison – but the story wasn't quite over.

Two months later, the shit is now in slow-motion, hitting my face and getting into my eyes. The new CEO at School of Rock corporate flew out to Palo Alto to hand me a termination letter. He had decided to terminate my franchise, which every franchisor has the power to do for certain reasons. I had mixed feelings when he slid that letter across the table. I loved the staff at SoR, they were some of the best people I've met, and I didn't want to put their jobs at risk. But I also felt it was time for me to go and just focus on theCoderSchool, which at that point was about 3 years old.

I applauded the CEO for making the right decision to cut me loose, to keep his system safe (or at least give that perception). It was the right thing to do for his brand, and the job of the CEO to maintain a clean image. But I resented his team and his lawyers for twisting the truth on that termination letter, saying things like I knew this was happening and that I knowingly hired a drug addict, none of which were true in the slightest. What I learned was that when something big like this happens, people go to their corners, ready for a fight. They do what's best for them, even if it means painting other parties in a bad light with untruths and false accusations. I decided right then that at theCoderSchool, if something like this happened, I would never fight a franchisee like that, and always do my best to support both sides. Win together, lose together.

A week later, we were hit by the lawsuit from the parents. I felt no animosity whatsoever about this lawsuit, and almost expected it by that point. Their child was hurt, and they were looking for compensation. I would have done the same. You never want to be hit with a lawsuit, but for this one, I felt ready. Felix and I had done our due diligence and documentation and, throughout the ordeal, had received plenty of support from our lawyers at the insurance company, all of whom felt we had a good case that this was something that we, as employers, could not have seen coming so were not at fault. But having a good case provides no protection from getting a lawsuit. Like many franchise lawsuits, they also pulled in School of Rock, the franchisor, because they typically have deeper pockets, if not just *more* pockets to take from. They would accuse the franchisor of not training me correctly, thus resulting in Jeremy being hired and, eventually, this incident.

Because I had been in constant contact with our lawyers from our insurance company, the details in the lawsuit were mostly expected. What I didn't expect was the amount they sued us for

– $18 Million. It's funny when that big of a number is told to you in a calm, robotic, and lawyerly way. In the end, it was much scarier than the result. Part of that is because of something called a limited liability company, or LLC. It means for business lawsuits, only the business' assets were on the line, not my personal ones like my house or personal bank account. Because I had one for School of Rock, and because I was soon to close it down after the school was terminated, it really had no value. The only value left was a $100,000 insurance limit that was used to settle the case. With no other options left for the plaintiff, the lawsuit was settled.

I've often thought back to see whether I could have known. Whether I *should* have known. The funny thing is, I knew Jeremy fairly well. He was a nice guy, and we'd go out to dinner sometimes. He bought me some tea from a trip as a gift. We bonded over his training for a marathon. Other people without any first-hand knowledge said I should have known, in an almost accusatory way. But to be blunt, what the fuck did they know – hindsight is 20/20. I've thought through the details many times, and even with a time machine, I still think that Jeremy's actions were entirely unpredictable. They just came out of nowhere.

Today, Jeremy has been released from jail, and he has since called all the people he impacted, including myself and Felix. He took accountability for his actions and apologized for how he impacted so many people while trying to rebuild his life once again. Because of Jeremy, I had lost my business. Felix, a great and passionate manager, had lost his job (and his business too, as I had given him 20% of the company by then). Our amazing staff were also impacted, some leaving the school shortly after. Worst of all, a child was hurt, something that can never be undone, and something we would never forgive Jeremy for.

Despite all that, our lives continued. It was stressful, but I eventually focused all my energy on theCoderSchool to build it to what it is today. Felix bought a house in a small town near the Oregon border and is now living his dream as owner of his own music school. I still have a great relationship with Felix and respect and thank him for everything he did for our school.

Felix and me (right) with two of my other insanely talented staff, Walt and Matt

There's a lot more detail to this incident that's too much for this book, but the gist of it is here. I started this section saying that this event had a significant influence at tCS, and it did. After this happened, I immediately created a super-structure of safety at theCoderSchool to try to prevent it from happening at tCS. This included a complex staff compliance system, more training, and strict repercussions for what happens when requirements aren't followed. And, as the CEO of School of Rock taught me, it also included the potential to terminate any franchisee due to safety reasons for the good of the system as a whole. We now have very robust policies, perhaps even moreso than School of Rock. While no structure can guarantee safety, I can say that theCoderSchool and its staff and students are much better protected than they would have otherwise been.

Part 4

Finding Our White Castle

Chapter 16

Getting it in Writing

In the Harold and Kumar movie, this is the part where they find the White Castle. They've been through their adventures, from hanging with the Asians at Princeton to meeting Neil Patrick Harris to getting their car fixed by Freakshow, and now they've finally made it to the destination they were looking for all along. They're ordering 30 sliders, 5 fries, and 4 large Cherry Cokes (or Diet Cherry Cokes for Kumar), because that's what you do when you finally find your White Castle. Whether you remember them getting there by riding a cheetah that's smoked too much weed or hang gliding down from a cliff, the result is the same – those two Asian dudes went through some great adventures to get what they had been craving all along.

And like those two Asians, we two Asians found our White Castle, too. Only it's not our real-life favorite fast-food joint, it's an analogy for the kind of business we've always craved since the rockstar days of Timmy Ramen. A business where we can spend our company money on dumb things like courtside seats at the NBA Finals while enjoying mundane things like White Castle together. A business where we don't have investors or bosses to pressure us to work harder to make more money. An impact business that's helping the younger generation vs. building big software systems for Fortune 500 companies (we'll leave that for our tCS kids to do). And best of all, a business where two best friends get to run it together and make their own decisions. theCoderSchool is *our* White Castle, and the bucket-list things that we now get to do are our thirty sliders and four large Cherry Cokes.

These last few chapters are about theCoderSchool life, our Great White Castle that we finally found, even as we continue our adventures. They're the bucket-list stories that make us feel like we've made it, starting with a common bucket-list checkbox – writing your first book.

First Contact

Not everyone gets to say they're a published author, but we can – even before this book you're holding. Back in late 2017, someone from England randomly contacted us about writing a book.

Dear Hansel and Wayne.

I am a book packager based in London and want to do a book series on coding for kids. I work with the illustrator Basher and I think his brand and yours would be a great fit. Basher's books have sold three million copies around the world (mainly in the US) and the brand has been licensed by Mattel to create a range of Basher Science Toys (currently exclusive to Target).

We get a lot of spam for all kinds of services to sell us all the time, but this one was different. This one was a legit service with a legit partner to do something we could check off our bucket list – being published authors. We excitedly and immediately set up a meeting with them, and it was as awesome as we had hoped.

Basher wasn't an illustrator we had heard of before, but now that we know about him, we see him in every bookstore. Back in 2006, he partnered with someone named Dan Green to create his first book, *Rocks and Minerals*, and has used this model of partnering with experts to publish over 50 books since in 20 countries, selling over 4 million copies by now. Toucan Books, the book packagers that contacted us, are essentially middle-men, folks who connect the content author(s) with the illustrator to put it into a book format for publishing. They don't publish the books themselves but rather shop them around to a publisher, who will buy the rights to publish them and send them along to bookstores like Amazon or Barnes and Noble. Of course, along the way, everyone gets some cut of the sales. Capitalism, right?

From the first email to finally publishing the book took almost two years. After we were first contacted, it took almost five months to decide what books we'd work on, an outline, and a few sample pages. Then it was proposed to the publisher, which took another 7 months to get a formal contract in place. After that, it took about six months to write, illustrate, and format the two books, another 6 months for the publishers to get the books distributed, and voilà, we were published authors! It's funny to think that in this process, the actual writing of the book only took a quarter of the entire timeline.

Kingfisher, a children's book division of Macmillan, signed on to publish our book. Macmillan Publishing is one of the "Big Five" of English-language publishers, so that was a big win – not every author can say they had a Macmillan-level company publish their book. With the publishing side of the contracts finalized, our book packagers at Toucan Books asked about our own arrangement. Like we said, everyone gets a cut. Well, almost everyone. We decided to respond that we didn't need any payment – the experience and brand exposure were enough. Part of it was that we suspected there wasn't too big of a budget (capitalism also means pennies for the little guy), and the other part was that's just who we are. That is, let's do something cool because of the experience and not the money – build some goodwill and see if it comes back to us in the long run. Toucan, in the end, gave us $1,000 anyway, as a small token of their appreciation. And no, we don't get any royalties on the book sales.

The Book

We wrote two books – one for younger kids about Scratch and one for slightly older kids about building websites. You can still find both on Amazon (search for theCoderSchool), though the Scratch book is now sold out. There's something like 88 reviews for the Scratch book, and 42 for the Website book, averaging 4.6 and 4.9 stars, respectively. Not bad for two engineers who had never written a book before. We didn't even have a ghostwriter;

the words in those books were purely words from our minds to those pages.

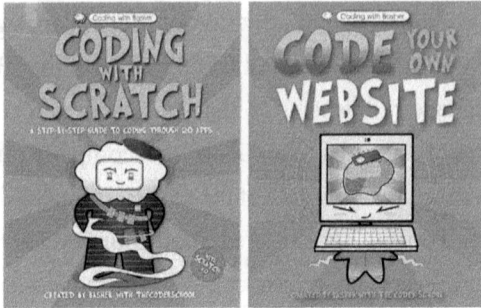

Our Basher Books

Technically, we ourselves aren't published authors – theCoderSchool is. This was something Hansel pushed for because it exposed the brand more than the name of two dudes you've never heard of. And we weren't theCoderBros back then (Hansel thought of that nom de guerre just for this book). We fought as best we could to put our official logo on the cover, but because it was a Basher book and part of his series, the publishers wanted to keep the same style, so they typed out "theCoderSchool" instead of using our logo. Wayne's dream of having his picture and bio on the back cover of a book was also squashed by the publisher for the same reason. But at least theCoderSchool name would be on the cover of two books that could be at your neighborhood bookstore anywhere in the country. And that was already pretty freaking cool.

On the day the book was published, we excitedly went to every Barnes and Noble we could to find the book and show our own kids that their dads were actual authors. But that didn't quite work out like we planned. We found Basher books of all kinds and kid's coding books of all kinds, but our own Basher coding books weren't there. Apparently, bookstores have buyers like any retail store – and they decided there wouldn't be enough interest for them to stock it on their shelves. They would all tell us, "But you can buy it online!" Helpful – not helpful.

Years later we caught up with Ellen from Toucan books, who hilariously told us something we already knew – our books did terribly. She said it wasn't the content or writing (yay, us!), but in her own words, "Who wants to learn to code with a book?!" It's a good thing that wasn't the core model for theCoderSchool. Even if the books didn't sell well, we still made the most of it by going on an official book tour.

The Book Tour

In November of 2018, almost 9 months before the book was even published, Toucan Books said that Macmillan was going to plan a marketing event for our two books in New York in the fall of 2019. They said they would pay for our hotel accommodations if we would fly ourselves out. We didn't hesitate for a second. Spending money to check an experience box is our thing, so we flew ourselves out to do a Book Tour for our own books. Sometimes you gotta pay-to-play for your bucket list.

The weekend of the tour was a blur. After a morning stop at a student assembly in a public school in Jersey City, we made our way to Short Hills, New Jersey. Short Hills is famous for being an affluent community, having made it to the Forbes Top 100 Most Expensive Zip Codes a few times. Canada's largest bookstore chain, Indigo, opened its first US location in Short Hills, and Indigo was the host for a book signing.

We pre-signed about 20 books like we were professional authors and waited patiently for the crowd. Alas, while we didn't exactly have a crowd of rabid fans show up, we did meet about 5 kids that day. It was cute, their dads would bring them up to us and say, "Go ahead, ask them to sign your book!" We're not sure if those

Hansel signs a book for a fan

4-year-olds really understood what they were doing, but at least someone bought the book! It wasn't quite the book signing that we pictured (it never is, is it?), with about 20 parents and kids in attendance, but it was still pretty cool to say we did it. How many people can say they flew to New York for a book signing? We left about 15 signed copies for them to sell on their endcap and went to our next stop of the tour.

Our next and final stop was more of the same but at a Barnes and Noble in the middle of Manhattan. Despite a smaller crowd, it was still a cool feeling to take over a section of the store, give a talk about the importance of coding to the crowd, and do a book signing in the middle of Tribeca, where celebrities like Jennifer Lawrence, Justin Timberlake, and Beyoncé/Jay-Z have homes. We never did see any celebrities in the crowd, but we sure did pray for that long shot. Oh well, there's always next time, right?

We wrapped up our Book Tour by having a great dinner with our New York franchisees and some folks from the publisher's team before Hansel flew home. Wayne, who missed the start of his family vacation in Europe, flew out directly from New York to France to catch up with them. And we both checked another pretty amazing thing off our bucket list – go on a Book Tour.

The Third Book

We don't want a book tour for this book you're reading – we've already checked that off. We're shooting higher – we want a movie! If anyone approaches us to make a movie, you can believe we'd pay to play that out. Like our first Timmy Ramen gig where we paid our way in, or our first books, where we wrote 'em for free, we work on the "relationship freemium" model. It's ok to negotiate against yourself sometimes and give more away to start things off. Show your generosity and your willingness to help the other side, right up front. You might find that people are inherently good and will give back to you later.

Our third book started with one of those many spam emails everyone gets. Unlike our first two books, this one was clearly an automated blast. This one was for Hansel and said something like "Have you ever thought about telling your story?" Hansel knew it was an automated email, but he was intrigued, nonetheless. He had recently thought about documenting his mom's life story as a gift not only to her but to himself and his brother Haniel, as a way to remember their mom's life decades later (he ended up instead recording a series of Zoom calls where she talks about her life – highly recommended for anyone with aging parents!).

Documenting his own story, though, sounded a little bit egotistical, if not just boring. Who was he but a random guy who built a company, like the millions of other people who have done it? But what if he did it together with Wayne? Then it becomes something a little unique – the story of two best friends who run a really cool business together. Wayne was on board quickly, and we were ready to go. So we started digging into how the publishing world works when you don't have a book packager doing it for you.

The Book Writing Model

Even though we had written two children's books before, writing a good memoir-style story is different. This one wasn't about teaching kids; it needed to be light and entertaining, written more as a story than as instructions for kids. This one probably needed a ghostwriter, someone who could take our thoughts and put them on paper in a readable format. And without a book packager, we also needed a way to get those words into a book format, get it published and up on Amazon, and do a little marketing, too. In short, we needed a whole turnkey package.

With a little research, we found two kinds of companies. Both had full package offerings, including ghostwriting, publishing, and even a little marketing, too. First, there are the real, legit companies that celebrities probably use to write their bestseller memoirs, which cost upwards of $80,000 or more, and use real publishing companies. Then there are somewhat fishy companies that are maybe legit but maybe not, are more in the $10,000 range, and have you self-publish your book. A publisher's job is to get the book distributed out there with some visibility to get sales. Self-publishing means you'd miss out on much of that or have to do it alone. We decided pretty quickly that as much as we wanted a memoir book, it wasn't worth $80,000. So, we focused on the second type of company in hopes they weren't a scam.

If you fall into the Google rabbit hole for these 2nd tier kinds of companies, you'll find they all look pretty legit at first. Great graphics, list of bestsellers, five-star reviews – the works. The closer we looked though, the fishier they felt. It seemed everyone had huge discounts like 75% off – that's a big discount for a legitimate service. Sites had authors like Dan Brown or Danielle Steele who used them – could those really be real? They promised reviews in the New York Times or LA Times – how can that be promised? In short, they seemed like they were too good to be true, and likely they were. We contacted a few to get some info, and the sales guys, surprisingly, seemed like pretty good guys. They had good answers for everything and made us think maybe they were legitimate businesses after all, but we still weren't sure. They even had a good number of 4- and 5-star reviews.

The quotes came in anywhere from $3,000 to about $30,000. That's a pretty big range for what's essentially the same service, which is part of the reason they felt fishy. They included a lot of extras like marketing – maybe *too* many extras. They had great video testimonials from authors – but we couldn't find any of them on Amazon. They had great reviews on Trustpilot – but we couldn't verify they were real. They had professional-sounding office addresses – but the address couldn't be found directly online. Strangely enough, many of the websites seemed fishy in the same way, with similar (but not the same) websites and similar (but not the same) responses and packages. It was as if it was one company that copied itself into multiple websites to get more visibility.

We kept going back and forth on which were legit, if any. Should we sign up for a $3,000 package that sounded too good to be true but would only be a $3,000 waste if it was a scam? Or pay $30,000 ($25k, actually – with a discount for paying upfront) for a company that had a feeling of being a smaller-time player, but felt a lot more real, and less like a huckster selling us? This company didn't seem like a copy of the others, the founder had gotten some press on some real media, and the reviews for the most part looked genuine and were 5-star. We took the bet and settled on this company, hoping and assuming they would be legit. If you're reading this book, then you can assume we made the right bet.

Ghostwriting

Once we got set up, our first step was to find the ghostwriter, who would help us put our thoughts to paper. They first give you a list, you meet them over zoom, and then you pick the one that fits you best. To be honest, the first 4-5 we interviewed were way off base. One barely spoke English, one ditched our zoom entirely, and one was a religious zealot. We were worried.

Finally, our $25k bet paid off, and we were connected to the great Jason Klamm. From his initial bio, we knew he was the guy. An accomplished author and director, an award-winning screenwriter and actor, voice actor, and even a podcast host. As if that weren't enough, he also wrote a book about 90's TV

Our First Ghostwriter
Jason Klamm

sketch comedies including some interviews with big names like Carol Burnett and Mike Myers called "We're Not Worthy" (hit up Amazon to find it!). That book title alone was all we needed to hear. He's probably got the cast of NewsRadio on speed dial and has met a lot of other big names in comedy, too. Most importantly, he knew and was a fan of the original Harold and Kumar movie. Jason was exactly who we wanted to ghostwrite for us. When we first met Jason, Wayne ended the interview by saying he could picture the three of us on a 3-man tandem bike, rolling through the hills. High praise, indeed.

To be honest, working with a guy like Jason was a bucket-list checkmark in its own right. He had a great personality, and we always looked forward to our meetings, where we'd shoot the shit while Jason cracked us up and wrote copious notes to put into book format later. But it taught us that being a ghostwriter is *hard*. Getting the intent of the authors through a single interview is damn near impossible. Did we say the right things? Did we forget some other things? Did Jason misinterpret our racist humor?

Real celebs probably have their ghostwriter living with them to write a legit memoir; there just needs to be that much back and forth. Our wives weren't quite ready to have Jason become our live-in ghostwriter, so we found a different way. Jason would write up a first draft with a skeleton structure and jokes we could use, then Hansel would rearrange it and add more detail, and Wayne would do a final read-through. It would get our hands deeper into the book and became a great way to streamline the process without having a ton more meetings to get all the info across and into the book.

Alas, it wasn't meant to be in the long run. Midway through the book, Jason unfortunately ended up with some personal things he needed to take care of and would no longer be able to help us with the book. We were super bummed, but as we do with anyone that leaves us for whatever reason, we wished him well and hoped we would cross paths with him again in the future. Maybe we'll team up to make this book into a movie and ride off into the sunset on our 3-man tandem bike.

Meantime, we had a choice to make. How do we finish the book? Do we interview more people and hope to find another Jason? That felt like a long shot at best, Jason seemed like a one-of-a-kind. So we decided the next best thing was to take control and write the rest of the book by ourselves. Hansel felt he had learned a lot from Jason in the first half and was ready to take on the challenge.

He would write the rest of the book with Wayne helping to proofread. It was like how theCoderSchool was built – Hansel would build it and create it, and Wayne would support it and help finalize it. The Yin was meeting the Yang yet again. This time though, we'd also add a Yong with Hansel's wife, Lisa, also editing this book for clarity and flow.

While writing this book ourselves is another great accomplishment, it's the meta-accomplishment that's the icing on the cake. That two best friends can shoot the shit and get down on paper all the stupid stuff they've been through – and do it all as a marketing expense, no less. That's living the good life, baby.

Chapter 17

The Good Life

Everyone has their own definition of The Good Life. Some want fame, others want wealth, still others want power. We want experience. It doesn't mean we don't want those other things; it just means our first focus is experience, and the other things, if they come, are a bonus. Two best friends who get to run a business that makes enough money to do some fun, random stuff together – that's our focus. Whether it's writing books or patting Steph Curry on the back, when you can do it on an expense account with your best friend, it's what we call The Good Life.

The Good Life, for us, also means a balanced life. theCoderSchool is a profitable enough business that we don't need to always stress about making that next dollar. Through 10 years of running a business together, we've had less arguments than you can count on one hand (it helps to have one friend who's a go-with-the-flow kind of guy, like Wayne). We have the time to stay healthy (Hansel probably spends 10-15 hours per week training for Ironman) or to travel (Wayne is a world traveler with his family). Our business impacts thousands of kids around the country every year, helping them prepare for the future. Best of all, we still have the time to be with and have fun with our own kids because in the end, The Good Life means nothing without family.

Throughout this book, we've joked a lot that we're cheap as shit, and it's true for most things. But when it comes to experience-spending, The Good Life flips that concept 180 degrees. We'll be throwing out some real dollar figures here, so be prepared as it might sound a little obnoxious – but we thought you might be curious as to how stupid we can be with our profit for the sake of creating memories.

Peyton Manning

It all started in 2016 with Peyton Manning, football's greatest of all time (yep, we said it!). Hansel was not only a big Manning fan already, but he was also a huge Denver Broncos fan since his days in middle school, when Mike Lovejoy, one of his few friends back in Iowa, introduced him to NFL football and specifically the Broncos. And in the last season of Manning's storied career, he was the Broncos' quarterback, making it all the way to the Super Bowl.

Manning had been injured all year and didn't play like his normal self, so just getting to the big game was pretty long odds. Actually, having his last-ever NFL win possibly be the Super Bowl, now those were insane odds (in all of NFL history, only John Elway had done it – coincidentally, also a Bronco). And for the first time ever, out of all 30 stadiums in the country, the Super Bowl would be held at Levi's Stadium, 10 miles from

Hansel's house. The stars were aligned, it was fate that threw us into our first big game, before even any Warriors game.

So when the Broncos won the game that got them to the Super Bowl, Hansel immediately called Wayne. "Wayne, we are mother-f'ing going to the Super Bowl." Hansel wasn't about to miss Manning's last-ever game when it was 10 miles from his house, and Wayne wasn't going to say no to going to a Super Bowl.

The tickets weren't cheap at $9,000 each. It was the first time we bought tickets like that, so it was a bit of a shock to the system. You never really get used to spending a big amount like that on a literal big ticket item. We'd always have to check the bank account to make sure there was enough or pay off the business credit card first to make sure we didn't hit the credit limit. At least they were great seats, at about the 35-yard line and as close as you'd want to be to the field.

We got the tickets from StubHub which charges a giant service fee, something like 20-30%. Wayne had a friend who worked there and could get a deal on the service fee, so we bought it through her (thanks, Ervinna!). She was even a Code Coach with us for a bit, so it was all in the tCS family. We were playing it a little loose with her job since that wasn't exactly allowed, so it was the last time we asked her. Come to think of it, second to last, there was also the Warriors game with Christian later that summer. At least she did get a heck of a lot of frequent flyer points on her credit card.

Meeting DeAndre Hopkins in our Manning jerseys

Before the game, there was a pre-event where we had VIP access to an empty Great America, the local Six Flags-like amusement park, with open bar and free rides. NFL players did all kinds of events in there, and we got to meet DeAndre Hopkins, one of the best wide receivers of the day. Hansel still has his signed photo with D-Hop in the photo holder, which was free even though those amusement park photos normally cost $30. Sometimes the pre-event is as good as the main event, when you get to see sports stars outside their normal element.

Right before the game started, Wayne went to take a leak in the stadium, and he ended up at the urinal right next to A-Rod, a super famous baseball player who started dating J.Lo the next year. He didn't shake his hand and he didn't sneak a peek, but Wayne was star struck. A-Rod was about the biggest name there was in baseball at the time.

The game itself wasn't eventful, at least not for the purposes of this book, other than the excitement of watching Peyton's Broncos take the win. After the game, we were basking in the shower of orange and blue confetti. We've been trying to meet Peyton in person ever since to sign the special Super Bowl jerseys that we bought for $150 each. It was a crazy start to the big-game spending – but that's all it was, just a start.

Six Years Later

We began this chapter by saying The Good Life spending is a totally different ballgame, and we weren't kidding. Six years after the Manning Super Bowl, we went to another Super Bowl, this one with the Los Angeles Rams in L.A., otherwise known as the land of celebrities and money. Fittingly, the tickets were almost *three times* the cost of the Manning Super Bowl. You might say it's the opposite of White Castle, or you might just call us stupid-insane. It was actually way out of any reasonable price range that we would normally tolerate – but Hansel kept saying, "Once in a lifetime, Wayne!" (even though we, of course, had already been to a Super Bowl in our lifetime).

Ironically, we weren't huge fans of the LA Rams, although Hansel did root for them that year. The draw was that it was the first time the LA team made it to the Super Bowl, and by pure luck (Super Bowl stadiums are pre-determined way earlier), they would be playing in their home stadium, the brand-new SoFi Stadium. We knew if there was ever an event that we could pay for to see and meet celebrities, this would be it. We'd always wondered how we could get into the after-parties at the Grammys or the Victoria's Secret Fashion Show parties. The Super Bowl in LA would be it – for an insane amount of money. Once in a lifetime, right?

Unlike the Bronco's Super Bowl, the Rams one included a premium buffet before the game. It wasn't exactly worth the extra ticket costs, but hey, inflation, right? That would be the most expensive dump we've ever taken in our lives the next morning. Next to the buffet was a meet-and-greet event where we met and talked to Marcus Allen, a legendary Hall of Fame running back from the old days. They say never meet your heroes, but he was the nicest guy you could imagine, asking us where we're from and who we're rooting for and everything. We even found Wolfgang Puck, who served us some of his paella as part of the buffet. Not sure how much he enjoyed slopping food on a plate in the hot sun, but it was a great photo op for us. All this before we even got into the stadium.

Inside the stadium, it was set up like a zoo for human celebrities. A path looped around the stadium on the inside, where you could look up and see all the *even more* expensive seats in private glassed-in suites right above you. That year, the Super Bowl was *the place* to be seen. Each human celebrity glass "cage" had someone you'd probably recognize. Magic Johnson, Cardi B, Kate Hudson, Sean Penn, Chip and Joanna Gaines, LeBron James, Tracey Morgan, Ben Affleck, Matt Damon, Ellen and Portia, Steve Kerr, Anthony Anderson, Cedric the Entertainer, even Urkel from Family Matters were all on display.

We got a selfie with Chris Tucker, who played opposite Jackie Chan in all the Rush Hour movies. Hansel gave him the Bruce Lee "waaaaaawwwww" just like Tucker did in Rush Hour, and he laughed (Hansel *may* have already been pretty drunk). Is that racist if the dude is Black, and you're the Asian making Bruce Lee noises? Probably not racist, but maybe a little obnoxious; still, Tucker took it in stride.

After the game, we got a selfie with Daniel Dae Kim of Hawaii 5-0 (and other awesome shows like Lost and Airbender) fame, and also a huge AAPI advocate. Being 2022, Asian hate was a big topic, so we appreciate everything he'd done and still does, and we were super stoked to run into him.

Clockwise from top-left:
Marcus Allen, Chris Tucker, Wolfgang Puck, Daniel Dae Kim

During the game, we sat right in front of Katy Perry and Orlando Bloom and had basically the best seats in the house – 50-yard line, 20 rows up. Little known fact: unlike basketball, the best seats for football aren't the closest ones; they're up 17-20 rows. If you're closer to the field, the entire team (and the roaming camera platform) is so huge that everything is blocked, and you can't see a thing. Plus, if you're in the right section, most stadiums allow you to go all the way down before the game starts anyway, to get a good view of players warming up. Very few people take advantage of that, so you're welcome for the free fan tip.

Some stadiums like Hard Rock in Miami even let you onto the field, right behind the team, during the game. We couldn't see a thing when we went, but Coach Mike McDaniels walked right by us, close enough for an easy dap. Or Mercedez Benz Stadium in Atlanta lets you get right up to the players as they walk out of their locker room. When we stood right next to a player like Julio Jones, we literally felt like midgets. Or AT&T Stadium in Dallas, where the players run through the exclusive lounge on the way to their locker room. Hansel high-fived Marcus Mariota from the visiting team as he was coming off the field after he won that game. Even with the best seats we could get, those games were a lot less – maybe around $1,000 per ticket. We've been to enough stadiums at this point where we could probably write a book about all the secrets, but we'll save that for another time.

Travel Life, Travel Wife

While attending major sporting events has been a significant part of our "Good Life" experiences, another tradition we have is doing all our business travel together. We decided early on that we'd bump our budget a little for every trip, so all trips would be done together. It doesn't matter if it's a trip just for Hansel to speak at a conference, or a school opening only Wayne needs to go to – we're both going. We do it because it turns work travel from something you might dread into a Guys Trip, into something that's Good Life-worthy.

Sure, when you travel for work at the start of your career, it's awesome. Free trips with free food, what's not to like? But when you get older, you begin to feel the drag of it. Waking up early, delayed flights, unhealthy food – all in the name of work. With co-workers, you have to put on a face, be professional, dress up a little. But when you make it a Guys Trip instead – now that's something different. You have a best buddy to banter with, someone you can let loose your farts around and tell stupid Asian jokes to. Not only does it make the travel more fun, it gives us an excuse to travel places together.

For our Miami trip, we landed early and got drinks in South Beach. When we went to our opening in Tribeca, we toured around in a helicopter to get a birds-eye view of New York City. When we hit St. Louis, we went back to our alma mater, WashU,

Hansel Gruber falls off the tower

to reminisce about the old days. And yes, we eventually did some work on all our trips, but when we're both around, we can tag team and support each other, reducing the stress for us both. Plus, we share a hotel room to have a 2-man slumber party every time, a pillow fight with down feathers flying and all (and to save some costs).

We've gone to the SkyDeck in Chicago, where you can step onto a glass floor 103 stories up and do the classic Hans Gruber pic. We looked a little stupid laying on the glass floor with a selfie stick, pretending to fall from Nakatomi Tower, but you gotta pay tribute to Die Hard

Pretending to Ding Dong Ditch at Peyton Manning's actual house

when you can. "Yippee Ki-Yay, mofos!" We've done Niagara Falls during a crazy snowstorm, been upgraded to a giant suite overlooking the Times Square New Year Ball Drop (not during New Years though), and taken a tour of Mile High Stadium in Denver, where they show you the inner bowels of an NFL stadium, like locker rooms and player entrances (hint, many stadiums do tours, definitely worth it for any football fan). We've even taken stupid selfies in front of Peyton Manning, Tom Brady, and Michael Jordan's actual homes (you know, in case they came out and wanted to suddenly be friends with us), and we didn't get arrested even once.

Another travel perk came from one of our closest partners, the Congressional App Challenge, a coding contest run by the U.S. Congress. We were invited to DC for the winner's event in the US Capitol building where Hansel was a keynote speaker. We even got a chance to meet Congressman Ted Lieu before he went onstage to speak as well. Wayne would speak there the

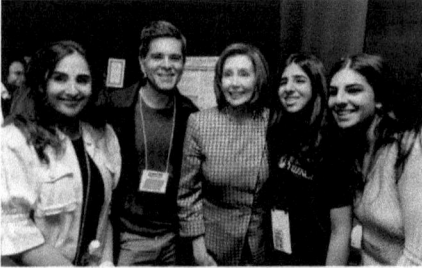

tCS student Shreya meets Nancy Pelosi

next year because he happened to be in DC with family, when Hansel wasn't able to (or was too lazy to) fly out. Some of our students have won the contest, too. In 2024, a student in our San Francisco location won, went to DC with her family, and met their rep – Nancy Pelosi. Whatever you might think about politics, it's cool as hell to meet one of the most famous politicians just because you can code.

A potential investor once offered Hansel free US Open tickets in New York. We weren't looking to deal, but free tickets to the US Open? Wayne is a tennis fanatic and even played in high

Happy to be at the U.S. Open for free

school with Ben Shelton's dad, Bryan, so this was a no-brainer. We found ourselves asking, "Would it hurt to listen to one investor?" The answer was no. Not when we got free tickets to one of the Grand Slams of tennis.

He was a great host, but honestly, we just thought it would be a fun trip since we weren't interested in an investor. When you're profitable and doing well, and especially when you're having fun, there's no need to get money from an investor. As Mark Cuban once said on *Shark Tank*: "Everybody thinks an investment is an accomplishment, but really, it's an obligation." Preach, Mark, preach.

There's only been a handful of times when we decided to travel without each other. In 2019, a school opened in Florida right around Thanksgiving, and Wayne couldn't make it. So Hansel spent a little extra to make up for Wayne not being there by flying first to New York, then to Florida, on business class, just to get a metric-ton of frequent flyer miles. It would be the first year he ever made 1k, the top frequent flyer status at United Airlines. If you're wondering whether getting to 1k is worth it, you get to board a little earlier and they give you a free $10 meal on every flight. That, plus you get to say you're in the top tier (actually there's an even higher tier for people who basically live on planes). So yeah, totally worth the $24,000 or so in airfare you'd have to spend in a year. Definitely, maybe.

But those trips suck, comparatively. Traveling in first class doesn't make up for traveling without a friend. Traveling with a friend, though, and going where you want to go – that might be the best part of our perks. Since we have locations (and potential locations) everywhere, we can decide to fly to almost any place in the country as a business expense. Gotta check in on those franchisees or scout out new locations in Minnesota, right? And while we're at it, maybe we'll have to take in a Vikings game.

In late 2021, we did one of these random trips. It was just after COVID, so we had pent-up energy, pent-up budget, and were seriously short on frequent flyer miles. We met up with our owners in Vegas, then took in a Raiders game in their new stadium. From there we flew to New York and planned on taking in a Nets-Warriors game. Alas, the good seats sold out, so we just watched it at Buffalo Wild Wings – go big or go buffalo, right? We probably burned around $7,000 for that useless trip just to get some miles and have some fun (and to check in on some franchisees). But when you don't have an investor asking where your money is being spent, you can be as stupid as you want.

The Real White Castle

The Good Life can be about spending up for stupid travel or crazy NFL games, but it can also be about how you spend your time together. The philosophy even extends to some truly mundane experiences, like our devotion to White Castle. We aren't joking when we said White Castle is our favorite – whenever we travel together on business, we seek out the Castle. Whether it's St. Louis, Detroit, Columbus (White Castle headquarters!), or good old New Jersey, where *Harold and Kumar* found theirs, it's our tradition to always find the Castle. It's not even enough to get a quick slider – we go for full-on meals, and often more than one time on a trip.

We're not exactly sure how this started. As simple guys, we've always had a taste for fast-casual eating, like Chipotle or Five

Guys, rather than sit-down restaurants. At some point in our travels, we probably landed in New Jersey late at night, both hungry, and ended up at a White Castle because it was the only thing open. That probably became a habit, and next thing you know, we're looking out for White Castle all the time.

There's also a mystique about it, too. The furthest west that White Castle goes is Las Vegas, so they're nowhere to be found out in California. When we went to WashU and when Wayne was living in the South, it wasn't like we ate that stuff every day. That's the problem with restaurants expanding so quickly nowadays – they spread everywhere and then they lose their mystique. Five Guys was awesome when it wasn't local; now that they're everywhere including near us, we never eat there. If there was a White Castle here in Silicon Valley, we'd probably think it was as greasy and gross as everyone else. Unless we watch *Harold and Kumar* again and smoke some weed, then we'd probably crave a bagful of sliders.

We've got a million of these pics

But for now, the only way we can get our sliders is when we travel – so that's exactly what we do. Well, they do have them frozen at the grocery stores, but who are they kidding. We recently stayed in a hotel where there was a White Castle about 2 blocks away. Needless to say, we ate there. In fact, we set a personal record. For a 2-day trip, where we had a real dinner with franchisees one night, we ate White Castle 4 times. With three meals a day for two days (3x2=6), and one meal being a franchisee dinner (6-1=5), we had a gutful of sliders for 80% of our non-business meals (4/5 = 80%). See? Math *is* useful. We'd like to meet any other idiots who would break that record. We'd probably treat 'em to... White Castle.

On another trip to New Jersey, we hadn't rented a car but got the craving. So we took an Uber to a super-sketchy White Castle 15 minutes away. When we pulled up, Wayne thought the

The Super Sketchy White Castle

group of scary-looking dudes outside was going to mug us. We got our sliders and got the heck out of there, taking another Uber back as fast as we could. We started to chow down in the car on the way back because you know White Castle sliders are at their best when the buns are still steaming, right? Sure, the driver probably gave us a terrible review for stinking up his car, but sometimes you just gotta do what you gotta do. We spent about $15 at White Castle, but about $50 on the Ubers. Totally worth it when it's tradition.

Semi-Annual Party

One of our favorite traditions is our semi-annual Coder Confab. The Confab is our big franchise get-together, a chance for us to hang out with our franchisee family in person. Usually called a Convention, ours is called a Confab because Hansel always needs to disrupt things, even if it's just the name. In any franchise system, this get-together is one of

What's up Dipali and gang! (our first Confab)

the most valuable things that come with buying into a franchise. The fact that our group of franchisees are mostly all amazing, supportive people makes it more like a family reunion and adds even more value. Not only do we get to socialize and have drinks with each other, it's real inspiration for them to learn from each other and hear how others who are just like them do the same thing they do.

COVID shot down our first attempt at a Confab – we had the Mirage in Las Vegas booked for May of 2020, which ended up being cancelled. It took two years before we felt comfortable enough to get into a group setting, so our first real Confab was in May of 2022 in Chicago. As great as it was to meet up with everyone, COVID shot that down, too – half of us had COVID after we got home. Hansel was out of commission for over a week. Even though we all tested beforehand and about half of us wore masks, the super-transmissible Omicron variant (remember that word?) was around at that time. Thankfully, we all recovered just fine.

theCoderSchool Family at the second Confab, a little bigger this time! (photo credit to Dipali, who lined us all up!)

Our second Confab was two years later, in May of 2024 at the Aria in Vegas. That Confab went exactly according to plan, and we were even able to hit White Castle twice on that trip. We took the entire gang of over 40 franchisees to the Sphere, that big digital ball (which, in our opinion, was a glorified IMAX theatre – not worth the cost), as a team bonding event since that was *the* thing to do in Vegas then. The Confab went so well that our franchisees asked us to have it yearly rather than every two years. At a little over $20,000 a pop (and growing, as more franchisees join) for us to spend, that's an expensive party to throw – but one that has some legit business value and makes much more sense than some Lakers tickets.

Jack Nicholson

After the celebrity-fest at the LA Super Bowl, we had to give it another try in 2023, this time at Crypto Arena, where the LA Lakers play. In fact, Lakers games have been historically famous for always having Jack Nicholson (and many other celebrities) at all the games. Although he had been absent for a while, we knew plenty of other celebs would be there. Our Warriors weren't looking quite as good that year, but they were in a battle with LeBron James' LA Lakers for game 6 of the Western Conference Semifinals. It was Steph Curry vs LeBron James, a matchup made in marketing heaven – all of basketball fandom would have their eyes on the game with two of the best playing. We had to go.

As usual, for the big games we went with the big seats – $10,000 per ticket. We weren't even on the first row of the court because those prices were out of range for us (they call it "celeb row" for a reason), but we were one row behind, and right at mid-court where the players check into the game. Not the best seats in the house – just the second best. We would feel some of that talcum powder Lebron throws in the air before every game with his legendary Chalk Toss and be able to look down Steph Curry's shorts when he stretched (not that we did).

Now, keep in mind that courtside seating is different for every stadium. The Warriors' home stadium (Chase) has two rows of seats on the floor for a super-premium experience, and five rows behind that which were "just premium" but also amazing seats, just off the floor. Both have awesome exclusive lounges with free food and drink, both have exclusive entrances, and both are first-class all the way. The only difference was that the super-premium lounge had more prime rib and sushi, and the just-premium lounge had more burgers and dogs. They treat you right at Chase Center.

Not at Crypto Arena in LA. The second-best seats in the house didn't come with anything at all. No lounge, no free food, not even a separate entrance (We had to enter the arena with the riffraff! What?!?). For the amount we paid, we were stunned. No lounge? No food? We asked a bunch of ushers, and they all said there was no lounge access, but we could order food from our seats. But hot dogs were still $15, so what's the point? That was enough to make us root against the Lakers forever.

We would sit next to a husband and wife who were also Warriors fans and went to every one of the post-season games that year (you thought *we* were burning money on tickets), including games in Sacramento. They said the same thing – Crypto is crap for premium ticket holders. It was funny though, because the husband was completely into it, high-fiving us and jumping up and down during the game – but the wife just sat there looking good, and sometimes bored. What an expensive way to support your husband.

As we waited for the game to start, we noticed this really old dude slowly sitting down with a few ushers helping out, in the seats right in front of us. He was clearly a VIP. It turned out to be Jack Nicholson, back at courtside after a long absence. He'd been out of the scene for a while, but he came back for this big game with his son. Wayne would work up the courage to tap him on the shoulder, tell Mr. Nicholson how much he changed how Wayne watched movies growing up, and actually shake his hand. It was an insane moment.

Wayne says hi to Jack Nicholson

That cool moment was followed later by a funny moment when Woody Harrelson, who was sitting all the way on the other side of the court, walked over to say hi to Jack. Woody was stone-cold drunk and walking through the basketball court free throw area, stumbling over while ushers tried to shoo him off the court (at least it was during a timeout). He was probably no more drunk than we were, but he had the balls (and the star power) to walk right in the middle of the Lakers basketball court.

During the game, Wayne got a text from an unknown number that said, "I just saw you on TV! Are you at the Warrior's game?!?!" It was cool as hell that someone saw him, but who *was* this person? Wayne didn't care, he just responded, "Haha, yeah, it's awesome!" without even knowing who it was. We'd later find out Wayne's face was clear as day on the TV, right behind Warrior's coach Steve Kerr, broadcast to over 8 million people during the game. Hansel wasn't on TV like Wayne, but we would later find out he was in a *People* magazine photo, right behind Jack Nicholson, who was in an article about his return to a Lakers game after a long absence. *People* magazine gets 77 million unique monthly visitors, so you could say Hansel got a 10x bigger audience. But no one texted him about that.

Wayne (upper left) on TV, behind Steve Kerr with Donald Sutherland (RIP) bottom right

The Warriors ended up losing that game and the entire series as well that night – their season was over. That, plus our spending a buttload of money on the flight and tickets and not getting free food or a private entrance made for a bummer of an ending. Lakers Suck! Or at least Crypto Arena does. It would be the opposite of what we felt the year before at Chase Center during Game 5 of the 2022 NBA Finals that inspired the Introduction for this book.

Chapter 18

In the Name of Bruce

◆————————◆

As the camera flashes continued to go off after the Warriors won that game against the Celtics in 2022, we had that deep feeling of satisfaction you can only get when your life is exactly where you want it. That game, that moment, was such a peak experience for us that we used it as our teaser at the start of this very book. When you buy seats that are right behind the billionaire owner of an NBA team with the money you made from the company you built, you know you've done something right.

We started that night with all-you-can-eat colossal shrimp and Manila clams with prime rib. Even if they had good stuff like sushi, chicken, or pasta, our job was to stick to the most expensive items in the buffet. Sashimi passes the test, but sushi doesn't because the cheap rice just fills the belly unnecessarily. Another secret to a premium buffet is grabbing as many free candy bars and jelly

Wayne goes to town

bellies as you can fit in your pockets to take home. Next time, we're coming with our fisherman vests with 20 pockets. The Chase Center's all-inclusive courtside seats also came with an open bar, so we started with Jack and Cokes. The other Asian secret here is to bring your Pepcid AC so your face doesn't get red.

We claimed our seats right next to Mike Breen, the famous NBA Finals announcer who yells "BANG!" when a big bucket goes in. He would yell it plenty that night for our Warriors. We would be sitting so close that Breen's TV partner would yell at Wayne later for trying to squeeze by him too closely as we returned to our seats after halftime. He wasn't famous though, so as stupid as we get, we still haven't been yelled at by a celebrity – yet.

We sat next to an older couple who were long-time season ticket holders. If you're not season ticket holders (like them), the only way you can get tickets is in a secondary market (like us). Prices in those secondary markets (e.g., Ticketmaster) tend to be a good deal higher than face value. As we started talking to the nice couple, the wife asked about our tickets and said, "Oh it must have been a fortune, something like $2,000?" Alas, she was off by a factor of 7.5.

We would get a selfie that night with Terrell Owens

Terrell Owens barely acknowledges us

(he was not the friendliest selfie taker), Chris Mullin (he was hesitant, but looked us up and down, and did it), and Festus Ezeli (super friendly, leaning on Hansel to give the peace sign).

NBA Finals Game 5, we're close enough to see Steph's "><" tattoo on his left bicep

If you don't know who these guys are, you don't need to – just know that the more famous they are, the less friendly they tend to be. Except Steph, who as famous as he is, still seems like he'd be the friendliest dude you'd meet.

That night, we would be close enough to Steph Curry to see the tattoo under his left bicep. It's two simple arrowheads pointing at each other, like "> <", a reminder for Curry to stay in the moment. If you ask Curry the key to his success, maybe this is it – elite athletes need to stay in the moment. If you ask us business nerds though, we have the exact opposite answer.

The White Castle Recipe

If Curry's tattoo is > <, ours would probably be < >, reminding us to focus not on the moment, but on the **bigger picture**. We think that's our primary recipe for success, and what makes theCoderSchool our White Castle. There were a lot of things that had to come together to allow us to get to where we are (chief among them – luck!). But if we were to pick just one, perhaps the most important key that we control is to always *focus on the bigger picture.*

The bigger picture works at many levels – for example, our company's vision statement (You did sign an NDA before reading our book, right?):

"Focus on the <u>best way</u> to teach kids to code, and collectively evolve it."

Our vision statement might sound like a bunch of generic corporate nonsense, but there's meaning behind it. Hansel long ago decided that tCS would teach kids in a low-ratio, custom teaching style because there is no better way to learn than to have an expert sit right next to you. Parents regularly tell us how much more engaged their kids are in our schools than at our competitors. Kids are also learning things they don't learn elsewhere – recently a Comp Sci major in college told us he was taught something in his college class that he had learned back with us when he was in 5th grade. Feedback like this reaffirms that our big-picture vision is guiding us in the right direction.

You'll notice there isn't anything in our vision about teaching the *most* kids or reaching the *most* communities – but our competitor's vision might. The Code Ninjas started after us but have probably five times as many schools as we do at this point. The original founder, David Graham, has sold the company, which is now run by an investment team. Kudos to him for hitting his own goal, albeit a very different one than ours. Two different visions, two different results, both obtaining a goal they set out to target.

The big picture applies to many other things. What do we want our lives to be about? We want great experiences. So let's get tickets to the NBA Finals instead of increasing our salary. Why did we write this book? To have fun, not to make money. So we'll probably buy a few boxes of books ourselves and give them away. What do we want theCoderSchool to be known for? Good people with good customer service. So let's bend over backward to help that student, even if it costs us more.

The thing with a big-picture goal is it often comes with sacrificing something else. Our vision statement talks about focusing on the "best way." But the best way is usually more costly, slower, and harder to scale – but we're ok with that, as long as we're teaching kids in the best way. Let's say your goal is to be the next Jensen Huang (founder of Nvidia). You can't be the CEO of the largest company in the world without "suffering," as he puts it, or sacrificing family time or social time to get there. Or take Jeremy Lin, two-time champion (once in the NBA, once in Taiwan). He had to couch-surf when he didn't know if the Knicks would sign him, and he travels a *lot* because of his sport and celebrity, so he doesn't have a lot of time for a normal life. Identifying your goals is a fun exercise – but don't forget the realistic sacrifices that come with them.

We all have different goals in life, in our businesses, in our relationships, and everywhere else. For us, the key to our White Castle success can be summed up in three steps:

1. Identify Your Big-Picture Goal – What do you *really* want?

2. Identify the Sacrifices to Get There – Are you ok with them?

3. Base All Decisions on #1 and #2

We've been fortunate enough to use this key to success over and over to build theCoderSchool into an 8-figure company (we think – you don't get a real valuation unless an investor gives you an offer). But who cares, right? Our big-picture goal isn't our valuation number. It's our experiences. And we've saved the story of our greatest-ever (to date) life experience as business partners for the end. You might think it's something like getting trapped overnight in a White Castle factory, but it's not. Instead, we turn to our other favorite – Bruce Lee.

The Little Dragon

If you don't know by now that we're huge fans of Bruce Lee, you've been smoking a little too much ganja. Considering the man died in 1973, it's incredible that we still talk about him as much as we do. When Hansel was growing up in Iowa, he would literally say "I swear in the name of Bruce" to himself whenever he needed to push himself to do something. Whether it was running that last mile or promising himself he'd stay up all night to get homework done, that was his go-to motivational phrase. We still have all kinds of Bruce Lee magazines from when we were kids and posters hung up in our homes. We know there's other big Bruce's out there – Bruce Springsteen, Bruce

Willis, even Bruce Campbell from *Evil Dead*. But to us, there's only one, and that's why we call him *The Bruce*.

Bruce Lee's favorite corner at his favorite Seattle restaurant, Tai Tung

We, of course, have done the standard Bruce Lee tour in Seattle, where he spent a pivotal part of his life. Highly recommended for all Asians (and other fans of The Bruce, too). Visiting Bruce Lee's grave that sits beside his son Brandon's – check. Taking a tour of the Bruce Lee exhibits in the Wing Luke Museum – check. We even ate at his long-ago favorite restaurant, Tai Tung (little known fact, oldest Chinese restaurant in Seattle), and ordered his favorite dish, Oyster Sauce Beef. Whether that is really his favorite or not, we don't *really* know, but since when has the Internet ever been wrong? We even sat in his favorite corner booth, at least that's what the staff told us. They could have told us he had a favorite toilet in there, and we would have taken a picture of us on said toilet pretending to take a dump.

The Bruce currently has two living immediate relatives – his wife Linda, who lives in Idaho, and his daughter, Shannon, down in LA. His son Brandon was tragically shot in 1993 by a supposed blank gun that instead had a lead tip in it when filming his last movie, The Crow (sound familiar, Alec Baldwin?). Shannon is a bit of a celebrity herself, having produced and acted in *Warrior*, the TV series based loosely on The Bruce's writings (great series – rooting for another season!). She also runs the Bruce Lee Foundation and wrote a highly acclaimed book called *Be Water, My Friend*, which tells the details of The Bruce's philosophy. She's also a parent like us, with a daughter currently in college. And every year (we think), she's invited to a special Golden State Warriors game on what their marketing guys call "Bruce Lee Night." If you can't guess where we're going with this, slap yourself awake, get a cup of coffee, and work on your reading comprehension. Otherwise, read on.

Meeting Shannon Lee

Author's Note: We get it, Shannon Lee isn't THAT big of a celebrity for most people. You probably couldn't pick her out of a crowd. But when you're huge Bruce Lee fans like we are, she's like a Taylor Swift or Ryan Reynolds in our eyes. If you find yourself not understanding the significance of meeting Shannon, global replace "Shannon Lee" with Jackie Chan, Michelle Obama, or your own favorite celeb and feel the magic along with us.

We don't usually go to regular-season Warriors games, but this one caught our eye. It was December 2023, and the Warriors were promoting their Bruce Lee Night. NBA teams often do promotions like these to get fans to come out during the regular season, and for this one they would give away a free Bruce Lee/Warriors poster. "What are the chances Shannon Lee would be there?" Hansel wondered to Wayne over email. It was her dad's night, after all, and we knew she had done some cross-promotions in the past between the Bruce Lee Foundation and the Warriors. Hansel asked a contact that worked with the Warriors whether Shannon would be at the game, but they wouldn't confirm (nor deny!) it. It would be insane to meet Shannon Lee – so we took a shot. As the saying goes, we put ourselves in the right place at the right time – but we also had to hope that we'd have the right amount of luck, too.

As per usual, we had to find good seats. What good would it be if we sat in the stands, and Shannon Lee actually showed up? So we got the best seats you could get in basketball – on the court, first row, right next to the Warriors bench. You can't get seats better than that. Lucky for us, they were playing the Detroit Pistons, at that time the worst team in the league with a record of 3-28. That meant the demand was likely lower, and we were able to score the best seats in the (still sold out) arena for a mere $5,000 each – Row AA. At the time, it felt like an expensive gamble. Especially because there were seats available only one row back in BB (still on the court, still at mid-court, just not next to the bench and not first row) for only $1,500. But it was The Bruce, so Wayne said let's make the big bet – first row seats. AA all the way. But would it be worth it? Or would it be a blow out game, where the crowd leaves early? Would Shannon Lee even be there? We were about to find out.

We got to our seats early as we always do and met Melvin, who was the usher (security is more like it) for the courtside seats. He was a friendly, stocky, black dude, bald with a big old greying beard, wearing his black suit with hands clasped in front. Put some sunglasses on him, and he could have been Secret Service.

Hey Melvin, let Steph through

Because our seats were on the court with nothing between us and the players, there were rules. Melvin said we couldn't walk onto the court's playing area, and we couldn't walk over to the bench, but we could try to high five players as they came back to their bench. We planned to take full advantage of that last tip.

The game hadn't started yet, so we went wandering through all the lounges and around the court, hoping to get a glimpse of Shannon Lee – if she was even there. We even asked some of the ushers and broadcasters – no one had any idea what we were talking about. "Bruce! You know, Bruce Lee Night, Shannon Lee?!?!" Wayne would scream to some very puzzled faces. The crowd didn't seem to be there for Bruce Lee Night either. Hansel was probably the only one wearing a Bruce Lee t-shirt (no, it wasn't the Game of Death yellow track suit, it was just a t-shirt). It wasn't looking like our gamble was going to pay off.

Then we saw her. Before every Warriors game, they have an on-court ceremony to ring a bell to get the game started. Shannon was the celebrity bellringer that night (who

Shannon ready to ring the bell

else, on Bruce Lee night?). As she walked onto the court, Hansel screamed "THERE SHE IS!!" to Wayne. We quickly ran back to our courtside seats right next to Melvin. The bell would be rung smack in the middle of the court, but Shannon was facing away from us as she did her promotional duty and took her photos with the Warriors crew.

We were going bonkers already, just because we were within about 20 feet of Shannon Lee. Keep in mind, by now we had already had a pretty good buzz going from the Jack and Cokes at the premium buffet. So Hansel, at the top of his lungs, yells "SHAAAAAAAANNNNNNNOONNNNNNN!!!!!!!!" about 5 times to get above the crowd noise. Melvin be damned, we started inching onto the court as both of us started yelling the name of the flesh and blood of our lifelong hero.

Finally, she heard us and turned around. Hansel, with his Bruce Lee shirt printed by the Bruce Lee Foundation that Shannon runs, started pointing at his shirt and yelling "Can we get a selfie?!?!" Looking back, yeah that's a little obnoxious-drunk, but really, you miss every shot you don't take – so we had to take it, obnoxious or not. Shannon was awesome and gracious, before she came over, she asked her Warriors handler if it was ok to come over for a quick selfie. We knew right then she was a down-to-earth, super-cool person.

She came over and we actually touched shoulders with her in the selfie. When you grow up with Bruce Lee as your religion, saying things like "I swear in the name of Bruce," rubbing shoulders with Shannon Lee was like touching royalty. Imagine putting your arms around the daughter of someone you've idolized for 50 years, memorized movie lines from, and even talked to in your head before going to sleep as a child. Surreal, dream-like, whatever you want to call it, that's what it was for us.

We were quickly jerked back to reality when, as soon as Shannon left, Melvin came over and admonished us – "That is the last time you fellas cross over into the court." We felt like school kids getting scolded by the teacher, but it was absolutely worth it. As we kept screaming excitedly to Melvin "Dude, that was Shannon Lee!!!" he had a wry smile on his face, thinking to himself "I better watch these drunk-ass fools closely tonight."

Satisfied that our tickets were worth the money already having met Shannon Lee, we turned to the game. It was a meaningless

Wait up, theCoderBros aren't in the huddle yet!

regular season game, so we weren't sure what the atmosphere would be like. It turned out to be a close game, and the crowd was as loud and crazy as if it were Game 7 of the NBA Finals. The next night would be a blow-out game, where the starters were pulled out of the game early, so the fact that the game was close was yet another stroke of luck for the evening.

Still, the experience wasn't quite over yet. There weren't any other celebrities at the game like you might find in the playoffs, but the players were pretty big celebrities themselves. During warmup, Chris Paul (you know, the guy in all the State Farm commercials that they call Point God in the NBA) threw his warmup tee off, and it landed right at Hansel's feet. So of course, he took it (stole it?) home.

As the game went on, we tried to take full advantage of the one thing Melvin let us do – give high fives to players as they walked off the court. Remember, our seats were right next to their bench so every time they checked out of the game they would walk by us, and every timeout had a player's butt about one foot from our faces. It was pretty cool to give a high five to Kuminga and Podz, both young up-and-comers for the Warriors. Understandably, the big stars like Steph, Draymond, and Klay were focused on the game, and didn't come close enough for a dap (probably on purpose, they'd get mobbed regularly if they did). But we did get to say "good game" to Coach Steve Kerr at the end and get a dap from him, so that's pretty darn close, especially for us huge fans of the Michael Jordan era. For you basketball fans out there, there is nothing like sitting in the first row on the court, it's a completely different experience than even the second row because there's nothing standing between you and the players. That BB row is for the riff-raff – AA all the way, haha!

As for the Warriors Bruce Lee poster that they gave out for Bruce Lee Night, it was an artistic drawing of Steph Curry in a layup, with a dragon swirling around him – pretty damn cool.

It was printed on thick card stock paper, not something you'd want to roll up, so we put ours flat on the ground under our seats. But by the end of the game, they were gone. We looked at the Indian family of four who sat right behind us and the dad had a stack of 'em, like 5 or 6, in his hands – so clearly he had taken ours as well, seeing them on the ground. Why anyone would need more than one, maybe two, is beyond us. But we have to hand it to the dad, he's teaching his young children well. It seems even Indians gotta Asian – if it's free, you take as many as you can.

To tell the best part of the story, we rewind back two quarters, just before halftime. The trick at any sporting event is to go back into the lounge a few minutes *before* halftime, not during halftime. That's because no one is there, and there's no line for food or the restrooms – everyone else goes *during* halftime when there's a huge line. If you watch any basketball game, you'll see that when they start the 3rd quarter, there's a lot of people missing from their seats – that's because they're stuck in line like suckers. It's all about efficiency, so about two minutes before halftime, we went to the lounge.

The lounge was empty as usual at that time. As we stumbled in, pretty buzzed, we saw a small group of people on the other side, and one was an Asian woman with a Warriors jersey on. Hansel yells, "Holy shit, THERE SHE IS!" loud enough for more than a few patrons to hear. It was, of course, none other than Shannon Lee, hanging out with her friends in the exclusive lounge. She's totally in the open, with no bodyguard team, no throng of fans, just chillin' with some drinks.

If we had been fully sober or even had any time to think, we probably would have turned away to strategize what to do (so yes, lucky for us, we were buzzed). But Hansel had already reflexively yelled out her name and even raised his arms in a "holy crap!" manner, and she had looked over, trying to see what all the commotion was. There was no choice – we were going in. It felt a lot like the old days when we'd get super nervous trying to work up the courage to talk to a girl at a nightclub, only this wasn't just some woman, this was the flesh and blood of The Bruce himself.

We walked up to her, and she was every bit as down-to-earth and cool as she was when we first yelled at her to get a selfie. That helped us relax right away, and our nerves faded away. We introduced ourselves, shaking hands, saying our names, and even telling her what theCoderSchool was about. She introduced herself and her daughter Wren, who was on her winter break from Tulane University.

We chatted like we were old friends for about five minutes – it was honestly a dreamlike sequence as we think back to it. We asked whether she watched her dad's movies (not for a while). We asked whether she comes to all the NBA Bruce Lee nights (she does). We asked whether she likes watching basketball (she doesn't). We even asked her about her show *Warrior*, which had just started streaming its 3rd season on Netflix. Its performance there would determine whether it would get a Season 4. We congratulated her on her success and her show, told her we were rooting for a Season 4, and joked that we'd go home and code something to fake-stream the show a million times.

After about five minutes, her friend came over and nicely said, "Ready to go?" to Shannon. We weren't sure where she was going, but that was probably her pre-planned rescue, in case some whack-o fans like us started rambling too long. Five minutes was the perfect amount of time anyway. Just enough time to talk to someone without saying something too awkward (Like "I used to pray to my Bruce Lee poster" – psycho fan alert. Or "You look great in that Warriors jersey!" – sexual harassment alert). In fact, after the conversation, Hansel would turn to Wayne and say, "Hey, we're both buzzed. Did we say anything stupid?" Wayne, it turns out, was well under control and said he was listening for stupid talk – and we both avoided it. Phew, catastrophe averted, likely thanks to that five-minute timer friend.

After the game, we tagged her on Instagram with some cool pics and said if she ever wanted to do a Bruce Lee Coding for Kids Week, we would drop everything and fly to LA in a heartbeat. Alas, she never responded, which is understandable for someone like her and a couple of random nutjobs like us. Perhaps one day, we'll figure out how to do a partnership with the Bruce Lee Foundation – that would be even more amazing than the night we had.

Still, that night left us with a lasting feeling, one that months later we would still fondly remember and say, "I can't believe we MET her!" Actually talking to the flesh and blood of our childhood idol is the unbelievable experience of a lifetime and a fitting climax for us in our still-ongoing story. The story of two Asian dudes who found this amazing life, who are now brothers forever, and who can't wait until the next time theCoderBros Go to White Castle. We're drooling already.

The Money Shot with Shannon Lee. We can now die happy.

Thanks

Special thanks to Hansel's Lobster, Lisa, for editing the crap out of this book, massaging the flow so it made sense, and adding about 1,000 commas. Couldn't have written it without ya! 😖 (the emoji is from Hansel, not Wayne...)

And thanks to both wives, Lisa and Winnie, for encouraging and supporting both of us throughout our adventures together. You guys are awesome – except when you're nagging us about the dishes.

Huge thanks and appreciation also to our entire Franchisee Family for trusting in us and theCoderSchool system, we owe you guys everything! In order of your first school's opening, thanks to:

Sharat, Kiran, Vinod, Srini, the giant ownership group that comes down to one dude – Brandon. **Will and Dede** - You're like family to us, LOL. **Dave and Lynna**, Go Card. Haha. **Luis**, so... you sticking with it or nah? We'll lunch again to find out! **Chris**, Should Dak really be the highest paid NFL player? Go Cowboys. **Jim, Lee, Allen, Irving** still waiting for our next dry-aged steak dinner. **Caroline**, thanks for Chinesing the Legal Seafoods bill every time! **Noreen, Zubair, and Nisha**, will you please open a school with more than 112 kids at the Grand Opening? **Jerry**, can we put up your picture after 5 locations? **Chad and Justin**, the memorable host of the Chicago Scene and the multi-tasking many-jobber. **Charu**, the sweetest and nicest of all. Can Beck sleep over at your house? **Marcel and Renata**, slow and steady wins the race, and you guys are winning it. **Vaishali and Chirayu**, why couldn't you get Jason Witten to come meet us at ESPN? **Noel and**

Danielle, living the Ninth Island life. **Umesh and Sanchayita**, you remind us of white snow, crazy cold, and of course, chicken wings. **Chris and Sherika**, missing your morning Timmy's, eh? **Chad and Ellen**, can't get enough of those jazz hands. **Dipali**, still want a job with us? Just kidding. **Derek**, thanks for flipping the ownership from a Chiefs fan to a Broncos fan. **Aline and Artur**, wow, that call that time you were about to move back to Brazil! **Kim and Malou**, turnaround King and Queen award! **Rajan**, ready to bring up the energy and fun level at every Confab. **Nicole and Denis**, always remembered as having your opening the day before COVID shut us all down. **Mike and Lesly**, as someone once said to us, you are "very New York". **Michael and Dom**, went thru some crazy, crazy shit with you guys re: that coach. Onward!! **Aditi and Rajiv**, ready to party at Elbo Room on our next visit. **Paul**, feels like we need another TV interview, doesn't it? **Tammy**, let's hope your next location doesn't take two years to open. **Teddy**, coach to manager to owner, what's next? **Emily and Rob**, we wondered why we were the only mask-wearers at your opening, heheh. **Nicole and Jon**, would have been hilarious to party with you guys in the clubbing days. **Anderson**, wait where'd Cindy go? **Shiv**, I'm sure all the rebranding work brought you great ROI (haha). **Francis**, the digital marketing king. E-sports at tCS soon, right?! **Fahad and Salman**, the most remote partnership there can be. **Jonathan and Jaimie**, love your mom on that first call, so Chinese!

And a preemptive thank you, dear reader, for not boycotting theCoderSchool because of this book. In fact, we hope it made you want to sign up with us. Even if you don't have kids.

Hope you enjoyed it!

9 798895 760314